Emersion

A Memoir of Addiction,
Incarceration, and Healing

e·mer·sion
/ə'mərZHən/
noun
the process or state of emerging from,
to rise above

Emersion

A Memoir of Addiction, Incarceration, and Healing

Edward Lee English Jr.

Book Design & Production:
Columbus Publishing Lab
www.ColumbusPublishingLab.com

Copyright © 2025 by
Edward Lee English Jr.

All rights reserved.
This book, or parts thereof, may not be
reproduced in any form without permission.

Paperback ISBN: 978-1-63337-944-2
E-Book ISBN: 978-1-63337-945-9

Printed in the United States of America
1 3 5 7 9 10 8 6 4 2

The story within these pages is a work of personal expression, shaped by my own experiences and thoughts. I want to make it clear that I do not endorse, support, or encourage the use or distribution of drugs in any way. Out of respect for the privacy and lives of others, I have changed some names throughout this book. Additionally, to protect the privacy of my family, I have chosen to limit specific information about them. Thank you for understanding.

Preface

As I reflect on my life, I'm reminded of all the turning points that have molded me into the man I am today. As I navigate through my journey of healing from addiction and incarceration, God, family, life, and death are all part of my transformation. These contributing factors have given me a deeper sense of purpose and understanding of life than I once had.

What started as journal entries during my addiction and incarceration have now become my memoir. This book is about the obstacles I faced while using and also while striving to become more than just another statistic from a relapse and incarceration. I have overcome many odds, and I'm reminded every day just how truly blessed I am to be alive. I believe there was a great shift in my mindset, which I will refer to as a second chance in life. In part, I believe I've been given this opportunity to live life to its true intended purpose, something my father and so many others who have struggled with addiction weren't able to achieve. From it, a call to write has emerged. Thank you, God, for being at work in my life and for giving me purpose. Thank you for quieting my mind and revealing to me the law of attraction. You have given me the ability to manifest all that is desired, and I truly believe that by drawing close to you, you have shown me my true potential.

What started as an idea has become something far greater: purpose. For those who dare to dream, dream. For those who have a vision, see it through. And for those who are unsure, take a leap of faith in yourself because no one else is going to do it for you. You can transform your life, and it's up to you to make that happen.

Thank you to my wife and soulmate, Shannon, for believing in me and supporting me through this journey. Thank you to my family, especially my mother, who has never left my side, and thank you to my close friends for never giving up on me. I dedicate this book to my dear friend Big Country, who saw the good in every situation and who had a laugh that was so contagious you couldn't help but laugh with him.

Contents

CHAPTER 1: The Meat and Potatoes 1
    POEM: Trippin 3
    POEM: Heroin 28
CHAPTER 2: And So It Begins 29
    POEM: Car Ride of Sorrow 40
CHAPTER 3: The Awakening 51
CHAPTER 4: The Transformation 63
    POEM: One Year Clean 85
CHAPTER 5: One Step Closer 87
    POEM: 33 & 3 97
    POEM: The Other Side of the Fence 98
    POEM: The Hole 110
CHAPTER 6: A New Way of Life 135
    POEM: When I Imagine 154
    POEM: From Your Eyes, I know 162
CHAPTER 7: Divine Timing 191
    OUTRO POEM 235

1.
The Meat and Potatoes

I guess I should start with where it all began to fall apart. It was the year 2000. I had just graduated from high school and moved to Sandusky, Ohio, with a couple of friends to work at Cedar Point. Working at the resort came with many perks, such as being able to go to the amusement park for free, which also included the water park and access to the beach. During that summer my roommates and I would often meet girls after work or go out on the beach as we were making the best of our summer on the lake. Many nights throughout the week and especially on the weekends, we went to the bars and clubs and out to eat. It was just a great experience for me as I worked with people from all over the world. One of the most interesting moments I had that summer was one night while out drinking. I found myself at a table playing a drinking game with a group of people from six different countries: Colombia, Russia, America, Uzbekistan, Poland, and Czech Republic.

This was the first time in my life I could say I experienced something like this. It was memorable because of the sense of freedom that it gave me. I knew the summer was going to be short-lived so I made the best of it. I wasn't a stranger to partying, and at this point I didn't have any drive to figure out what I was going to do with my life. My two roommates, Tony and Lewis, already had their minds made up on what they were doing at the end of the summer. They were just counting down the days before they moved to Pittsburgh for college. I, on the other hand, decided to stay in Ohio a little while longer with plans of returning to Cedar Point the following summer. The difference between me and those guys was that even though Tony and Lewis smoked a little weed and drank, I was more on the wild side, taking acid and ecstasy. It was around my sophomore year that I started getting into these harder drugs, so Cedar Point was just a summer-long party for me, and I loved it.

Like I said, I was no stranger to partying; it was how I found my sense of belonging, through socializing. It was during those early years that I found myself asking deeper questions about life. In my opinion, as I look back on it all, I was clueless and lost in life as I struggled to figure out my purpose. There was no clarity about those questions; I just remember being filled with more unanswered questions. The most valuable insight I had amid taking acid was a deeper sense of importance to life, even though at the time I couldn't put my finger on what that actually meant. I can say that I always thought I would find the answers to life at some point. But after high school, I had no vision or clear plans of action, which is why I stayed in Ohio one more year.

My biggest goal in life after high school was to turn twenty-one so I could buy my first keg. My first summer at Cedar Point was special because I was away from home for the first time, but nothing prepared me for what was to come the following summer.

Trippin

My mind divides pink clouds and lavender skies
while the sun starts to rise.
As waves crash the shore I realize they are tiny bubbles
and nothing more.
Visions are still in my head from the night before.
Glow-stick ink stained on the walls,
Botticelli wallpaper came to life as the plants grew
on the haunted carpeted halls.
The sun is on the horizon and a part of me is at peace.
The hallucinations are over and my mind is at ease.
The past few hours I spent on a colorful, vivid trip.
Ten years have gone by and I'm still making sense of it.

I spent my second summer at Cedar Point with another close friend of mine, Shane. We had a history of doing crazy things in high school together. One time in high school Shane and I were with a group of other kids, partying in the country. We found a country road surrounded by cornfields, where we parked and started drinking and taking acid. I can't remember whose car it was that we jumped in, but it was a Mustang 5.0 convertible, and we were tripping on acid. We drove back into town to go to the drive-thru for orange juice and cigarettes. As we got there, we had the top down, and Shane was standing up in the back, losing his mind and laughing like a mad man, screaming about wanting a Yoo-hoo and Starbursts. It was so hilarious that my face hurt from laughing so hard. As we got back out to the country where we were partying, he had the bright idea of riding on the hood of the car. I can't remember who was driving. All I remember is that Shane kept saying he wanted to ride on the hood of the car as we got closer to the spot we were hanging out at. As we got closer to turn off the road into the cornfield the car slammed to a halt and Shane flew off the car into the cornfield. The whole group of people we were partying with lost it. I mean everyone was laughing—even Shane came out of the cornfield laughing. He had to have flown close to twenty feet from the car. It truly was a scene.

We were a lot alike in how we approached life. We both were very high energy. Shane brought the best out in me in ways I couldn't understand back then, which is why I enjoyed being around him so much in high school. Deep down I was reserved, but he was funny, and once I got out of my shell, I was able to forget the lack of confidence I had in myself. We were close like brothers and even fought like brothers. We were carefree, adventurous, and definitely too much to handle once we were around each other for too long. My summer with Shane really deepened our friendship all the more. We lived in the Hotel Breakers at Cedar Point and had a dorm room to ourselves.

After about a month we got the bright idea to see how long we could go with keeping the room to ourselves. We agreed upon a plan to chase off any potential roommates. "How?" you might ask. Well, we pretended we were nudists in the privacy of our dorm. The first unsuspecting soul never lasted a day. That first afternoon when I came back to the dorm from work, Shane was sitting at the table in his boxers with the new roommate. The guy hadn't unpacked yet. As I walked in, Shane had the look in his eye to initiate our plan.

I started talking to the roommate, asking general questions. I went into the bathroom and started running the shower. I came out, got naked and walked across the room, all the while carrying on the conversation as if it was our normal routine. You could tell the guy felt awkward; he wouldn't make eye contact. I finished my shower and came out of the bathroom naked. While drying off, Shane dropped his boxers and grabbed his towel, went into the bathroom, and started taking his shower.

As Shane was showering, he yelled from the bathroom to the potential new roommate. Oh yeah, I forgot to tell you, we don't keep our clothes on after work. Right when Shane said that I turned around while standing at my bed, hiked my leg up onto the chair on the other side of the table, and started drying my inner thigh. The guy said, "Yeah, I'm good with that. I can get another room." He grabbed his bags and left. We thought it was hilarious. The whole situation lasted thirty minutes tops. I ran into the bathroom and said, "Holy shit, it worked—he left!" The next morning we were called into the manager's office. They asked about the incident from the night before. We merely replied, "Well, we didn't want to put our personal business out there. This is why we requested to dorm together. We're nudists." We never had another roommate for the rest of the summer.

It wasn't too long after that incident that Shane met a guy while working who offered him an opportunity to make some extra cash. We were paid to drive to festivals so the guy could sell AMT. The people we got the AMT from didn't have transportation, and I had the car and the license so it worked out in our favor. We had several road trips together during the summer of 2001. Our trips consisted of going to music festivals and experimenting with hallucinogens. AMT was the highlight of our summer, and the people we knew had what seemed like an unlimited amount of it at the time.

AMT is a synthetic hallucinogen, and at the time it was technically legal. It wasn't listed as a scheduled drug until 2003, which meant that if caught in possession of it, it wouldn't come up as a classified drug. Because of that, we found ourselves a little more carefree. Our experiences taking AMT would last for up to twelve hours at a time with very intense visuals. For instance, I was at an ekoostik hookah music festival, and I was completely overwhelmed with an intense body buzz. I lost track of time—and at one point it was daylight, and then it wasn't. I couldn't remember the sun setting.

I looked up into the night sky toward the tree line of the tall pines. They were melting upward into space with vibrant rainbow colors. I couldn't believe my eyes. The colors were so peaceful, but the trees were swaying violently side to side. I was confused but at peace. Eventually we found our way out of the festival and back to my car, where I spent the rest of my trip listening to the Grateful Dead and Pink Floyd. As morning came I was ready to head back to Cedar Point. I felt like I had time-traveled back to the '70s or something.

My first festival made a lasting impression on me. I just looked at it as a journey. It was during this experimentation phase of my life that I came up with the poem "Trippin." One night the wallpaper in our bathroom came to life while I was hallucinating. The leaves from the Botticelli artwork floated across the wall as the hair on Venus's head came to life. If you're not familiar with Botticelli's artwork, let me explain.

Botticelli was an Italian painter of the Early Italian Renaissance and can be found in museums and galleries in Florence, Italy, and also Paris. The subject of most of his paintings was the goddess Venus, which postured beauty and virtue. So now that I've shared with you a little art history, hopefully you have enough information to paint a picture (no pun intended) of what I was seeing while hallucinating. The wallpaper was of the birth of Venus. As she stood naked in a giant clamshell, I saw that her hair was long, covering her nudity and moving fluidly. The breath from the angel in this scene was blowing flowers and leaves through the air, and they were moving across the wall. The water in the background came alive, and the waves were washing ashore. The cloak that was being held from what I assume was another goddess was also flowing effortlessly in the wind from the breath of the angel.

I was stuck in the bathroom for a good two hours, according to Shane. I took the AMT with Shane about a half hour before I got in the shower, while smoking a bowl of weed. He left to go meet a girl before we went out for the night. Midway through the shower the AMT kicked in, and time literally slowed down for me. The water coming out of the shower went silent, and the water droplets left sound-wave trails right before my eyes. I began to get out of the shower, and that's when I saw the wallpaper come to life. I sat down on the toilet, soaking wet, smoked a cigarette, and just got lost. It felt like twenty minutes had gone by, but when Shane got back he came into the bathroom and started laughing his ass off because of the look on my face. He knew I was tripping.

As our night continued we decided to get out of our apartment and explore the hotel and beach area. While walking in the hallways to the hotel, the decorative ivy on the red carpet started to grow in the halls. The hotel doors in the hallways appeared to turn into an infinite hallway to nowhere. I was convinced that the original part of the Cedar Point Hotel, Hotel Breakers, was haunted because of those hallways. Eventually we made our way back to our room as I was eagerly anticipating the end of my trip.

Some of my craziest trips were from that summer, but this night specifically left me with some of the most vivid experiences. As the trip wore off, I remember sitting there looking at the condition of our room. With glowstick ink flung everywhere, the black lights in our dorm illuminated the chaos we classified as a journey. I needed to clear my head and made my way out to the beach, where I took my shoes off and walked the edge of the shoreline while watching the sun come up.

Most of our road trips took place over the weekends. We would leave Friday after work and be back by late Sunday night to start work again on Monday morning. We went as far north as Michigan to the Detroit Electronic Music Festival and even went into West Virginia, following music festivals. Eventually our road trips ended, and the people we were driving to these festivals with were headed further west. Shane and I didn't intend to go that far so we parted ways from the group, only to return back to Cedar Point to end our summer.

As I look back on everything now, would I have done things differently? I'm sure I would have. However, they wouldn't be a part of my story today.

As quickly as our summer had started, our time at the lake had come to an end. A few months after coming home from Cedar Point, nothing had really changed. I was still taking ecstasy and acid and even experimented with mescaline. At some point I remember talking to Tony on the phone about Pittsburgh when he suggested I move in with him and Lewis. His invite was focused around the opportunities that the city could offer in comparison to my hometown's economy. Back home, the only employment possibilities were restaurant and factory jobs. "I thought about it and figured, what could it hurt?" Worst-case scenario, if it didn't work out I could always move back home.

 I began to consider my options and found the Art Institute as a possibility. After applying to the school I was surprised that the school accepted my application for the Audio Video program. I had a feeling of surprise because I had no experience with editing or camera operation. The school recruiter advised me that I would get all the training needed to be successful in this field. I never really had any set goals, just a list of interests. I went to the Art Institute because I liked music, and I enjoyed watching TV shows and movies. At the time I believed this school was my ticket to being successful.

 Once I moved to Pittsburgh I took a tour of the school's labs and media department. It was amazing, and I actually felt motivated during this process. I decided to take the opportunity and signed the papers, and it didn't take very long before I fell into a routine. In Pittsburgh, while I waited for school to start, I would frequently stop by to socialize and get comfortable with the layout of the school. I figured out pretty quickly that the majority of the students liked to party, which was good for me because I loved partying.

 Tony was selling weed, and for me as a college student now, I knew there was an opportunity he couldn't turn down, which was more clientele. It was a perfect situation: I sold for Tony and I got to smoke weed for free. Eventually I got housing in the dorms on the North Side of Pittsburgh. This gave me access to more students, so naturally moving into the dorms was an opportunity worth taking. The amount of weed I sold brought in enough money that I didn't need to work. Even though the extra money was nice, I kept a job. I worked at a little cigarette shop downtown where I ran the lottery machine and sold cigarettes. It wasn't a bad gig for me. My cigarettes were on credit, and I got to meet people. What more could I ask for?

While living in the dorms I quickly made friends with a group of people who had similar interests as mine, such as street skating, partying, and music. We often hung out in each other's dorm rooms making food, ordering pizza, and doing things in the city together. We would skate and make videos of our tricks along the river and downtown, jumping staircases and other stunts. We would walk around the downtown streets, exploring the different stores and the cultural food district that Pittsburgh is famous for.

The food scene was like nothing I had ever experienced before. Seeing freshly made bread and mozzarella cheese being made by hand right in front of you was appealing. Diners that shared their history with black-and-white pictures hung on the walls told stories of a time before I was born. The city of Pittsburgh was rich with history, from pro and college sports teams to buildings and businesses dating back to the original steel-mill era. My time in Pittsburgh was just getting started, and already I had grown to love this city.

It wasn't long after moving into the dorms that I and a few of the guys I hung out with decided to get our own apartment. By the end of July I had what I could call my first place. The house was sketchy to say the least, but it didn't matter because it

The Meat and Potaotes

was ours. At first glance the house spoke of a darker side to the neighborhood. It was attached to the side of a rundown bar. The color of the house was a yellow aluminum, faded from years of weather exposure. The yellow was dingy and felt depressing when you looked at it.

Some missing sections of siding were replaced with mismatched white siding. Just like the exterior of the house, the same went for the inside. Residing in a rundown area on the North Side, the house had brown carpet and wood paneling on the walls. The house was a three-bedroom, one-bathroom structure with a makeshift shower in the basement that was really more like a dungeon. The house hadn't been updated since it was first built, but we didn't care because the rent was cheap. It gave us more freedom to party, which led to more drugs. The proper term for our landlord would have been "slumlord." The apartment was convenient to downtown and to the school.

If you decided to walk to school you could get there in the same amount of time as if you were walking from the dorms. The most convenient thing for me about the new apartment was that Tony and Lewis were less than twenty minutes walking distance from me. It was nice having acquaintances from my past living in Pittsburgh, because I didn't feel completely alone. One night while partying at Tony's apartment, I remember trying OxyContin for the first time. That night, using OxyContin changed something in me. I had never felt anything like the effects that that little pill had on me. At this point from all my drug usage, it was safe to say I felt comfort within that pill.

All my concerns drifted away when it kicked in. There was a comforting feeling associated with it that I compared to ecstasy but far more intense. I was numb inside but I also felt warm. It was as if it had touched my soul in some way. I was clueless about the effects of this drug. At the time I didn't know much about opiates or about heroin being in the same category.

Seeing either one of us, me or Tony, for the first time, you would never know we were into using or selling drugs. Both of us were well-dressed, well-mannered young men. I guess it was a reflection of a different time regarding how we were raised. Tony was in really good health and came from a sports background as a kid. He played football, which he was really good at. He was a good-looking guy with a great smile and had no issues talking to girls. He always had a girlfriend. I looked up to Tony in many ways, as I did Shane. I could trust these guys, and I knew they had my back if anything ever went wrong. Tony wasn't shy and carried himself with confidence. I felt that being around Tony brought out a piece of confidence in me as well. I had low self-esteem and lacked confidence, which in part played a role in me being somewhat of an outsider during high school. Now as I was getting older I felt that I was breaking out of my shell. I became more self-reliant, and I had my friends to thank for that.

In high school Tony didn't hesitate to share his opinion about things. I was able to feed off that. Being around Tony gave me exposure to peers that I may not have had an opportunity to be around otherwise. In many aspects I wasn't as confident in comparison to some of the other kids I knew growing up, and you will learn to understand why later on in the book. It was because of guys like him that I was able to find the courage to spread my wings and embrace who I was as a person.

The Meat and Potatoes

The feeling from OxyContin was so strong that I believe it reprogrammed something in me, and I couldn't stop obsessing over the first time I used it. From that night on, the feeling and wonder about using it again nagged at me for weeks. It was about a month later I came across an opportunity to try fentanyl. My exposure to so many students in the dorms while selling weed and partying allowed me to learn about fentanyl. I was told it was like OxyContin but cheaper and stronger.

Being in Pittsburgh was still new to me, and now I was being exposed to a whole new underworld of drugs. The fentanyl was packaged in little wax paper bags called stamp bags. My first time using it was with two girls, Mia and Amelia. Looking back on that first time I did a stamp bag, I recall that it didn't take much. The amount was only about the size of the white tip on a matchhead. It took me right back to the night of using OxyContin. The same feeling came back again, and as euphoric as it was, it didn't occur to me that I was trekking down a dangerous path I'd potentially never return from.

Until now everything I had chosen to do in life felt like I was in control of whether or not I wanted to take a break from partying. I had no idea I had opened up a whole new set of problems using opioids. The stamp bags were popular, and I wasn't the only person getting high at the school. There was an underbelly among the students at the Art Institute. If you knew who they were then the stamp bags were easy access. If not, well, you just never knew about the bags. The two girls who offered me my first stamp bag were Amelia, who eventually became my girlfriend, and her sister, Mia.

Both these girls were beautiful in their own unique ways. Mia had short, auburn-dyed hair and several tattoos and piercings. She was more on the darker side when it came to what she liked to wear. She was more of a skater/Goth type, but she also embraced the candy-kid vibe with her bracelets and necklaces that most girls wore at raves. Her appearance may have been taboo at the time, but it was overlooked because of her smile and personality. Mia was a sweet girl and could talk to anyone, and I loved that about her.

Her sister Amelia was just as beautiful, yet the exact opposite in appearance. She was reserved and preppy. She had blonde hair and blue eyes with no visible tattoos. Both girls were very smart, and we all seemed to share similar interests. Early on, I enjoyed spending more and more time with both girls. Eventually the dark truth came out that both girls were snorting fentanyl. The first time I tried fentanyl was in the fall of 2003, I would say three to four months after I had first tried OxyContin.

One night, I offered Tony a stamp bag while we were meeting up so I could pay him for more weed. He got pissed and said, "Man, you're doing heroin, dude—what the fuck?" I told him it wasn't heroin; it was fentanyl. He reassured me that the two were the same thing. That night I called the guy I was buying the stamp bags from and explained to him what I had found out, and he said yeah—OxyContin, fentanyl, heroin—t's all the same drug. They were just different versions, but one was stronger and the stamp bags were cheaper. Tony and I got into an argument because he called me a junkie, and it didn't sit well with me. Personally, I was at a loss for words. I was scared, and I panicked within my own thoughts, because the last thing I was trying to do was become a heroin addict.

Looking back on it all now, I can say the worst mistake I ever made in my life was getting into opiates. There I was, out there in Pittsburgh using heroin. I had just gotten into an argument with one of my close friends about it, and just like that my bright future had turned cloudy. I could feel the shift in energy. I didn't know what to do. I felt my perception of everything change right before my eyes. The world just got dirtier it seemed. Personally, I refused to admit to the accusation that I was a junkie. I found myself justifying one day a week as not being a junkie.

It seemed as though there was still time to change things around, and inside there was still hope to control it. How could I be an addict? I was in college, I had a job, I thought I was all right. Little did I know I was rationalizing my actions, and I sure as hell didn't realize at the time I was lying to myself that using was okay. After all, once a week wasn't anything to worry about, right? I drank and smoked weed more than I used this.

I thought to myself, *it's funny how life goes on even as you've accepted your own failures.* The ability to adapt through acceptance truly gives you insight into just how powerful our minds can be. We are more in control of ourselves than we are led to believe.

As I was confronted with this revelation in my life, I found myself feeling alone despite the fact that I was in a relationship with the girl I was getting high with. Even though I had tried the fentanyl for the first time with her and her sister, this wasn't about blaming anyone. These were just the facts. I was doing what felt right to me at the time, and doing drugs was what felt right. It was welcoming, and it's where I felt comfort. When doing drugs, I was around people who made me feel accepted. My idea of what love was kept me comfortable with staying in the relationship with Amelia. Because of that, I continued to get high in an effort to avoid the fear of breaking up and the judgment from others.

Within a few months, my boundaries around using fentanyl once a week turned into Wednesdays and Fridays. By the time my first year in Pittsburgh was up, I was using three or four times a week. Financially I was fine. The bags were only six dollars apiece. I was still selling drugs, and things seemed good even though I was spending less and less time hanging out with my roommates. I eventually moved out about six months after getting the place with the guys.

I moved in with my girlfriend and her sister, and that following year things started to change. In spring 2003 I woke up from what felt like a short nap. It turned out to be several hours of nodding out from being high. I just lay there and stared at the ceiling. There were cracks on the walls and ceiling from the old house settling over the years. The apartment was in disarray because we were in the middle of moving again.

I had this overwhelming sense that something wasn't right in life, and I started to get concerned. This wasn't just me being paranoid, though; these were feelings of uneasiness. I started thinking about my life and the fact that I was still using dope. Then I began reflecting back to the last time I had talked to Tony. I couldn't believe one year had gone by already. You could call it intuition, because I knew I needed to stop using. I told myself I was done, and I was, but it was only for about six weeks or so. Just enough time so that things in my life felt okay again.

I still had people calling and asking for fentanyl, and I kept telling them no and that I was done with that stuff. It seemed like they just didn't believe me. I didn't understand it at the time, because I never actually got dope sick. People would always ask me, "You don't get sick?" I just didn't understand what dope sick was. I remember one night at a house party one guy told me, "I can't believe you've never gotten dope sick." He then said, "You'll know when you're sick—that's when everything changes."

While I lived in Pittsburgh a lot of the people I hung out with were big into the rave scene, and I was occasionally going to raves and selling ecstasy. Along with acid I was also eating mushrooms, but my drug of choice was always fentanyl. I met quite a few people in a short amount of time, and a few were DJs trying to make a name for themselves through music. I traveled to Cleveland and Canada to watch them play and even had VIP passes a couple of times for the parties. A few of the people I partied with could get ecstasy from Canada, so I would put my money with theirs, and during those trips to Canada we would buy ecstasy and then bring it back.

It wasn't a lot compared to some people, but to us five hundred to a thousand pills was a decent amount of money. Once back in the States I would sell the pills to people I knew and at parties in Pittsburgh. We called raves "parties," and a lot of times I wouldn't even know where the parties were until an hour or two before they started. Empty warehouses and airport hangars out in the middle of nowhere were usually where we would end up partying. I didn't know how these events were put together, but from time to time some of those events actually had decent production behind them. It allowed me to see some really well-known artists.

Even though my time in Pittsburgh was relatively short, it still seemed to be a blur for the most part because of all the drugs I was using. I do know that I really didn't start selling stamp bags until about one year after I first started using fentanyl. So much happened in a short amount of time. Amelia moved back to

Cleveland for college, and Mia stayed as my roommate because she was in photography at the Art Institute. By the end of spring 2004, I found out that Mia had dropped out of school and was shooting dope. At first I panicked because I was worried about her. The selfish part of me feared I was going to get blamed or something. Amelia had her family get her sister and take her to get help.

My final year in college was quickly approaching as I entered my last eighteen months of school. I was beginning to work on my final projects and presentations before the 2004 summer quarter break. My friend Shane came out and stayed with me for a short while right as summer break kicked in. You would think that after Mia moved home to get help because of her heroin addiction, I would have stopped using. However, the never-ending feeling of just one more time plagued me as a constant reminder. That plus the people who were asking if I could get dope was more than I could take in.

While Shane was visiting Pittsburgh, my heroin usage got him into using. It turned his stay into a train wreck of an experience. As nice as it was to have one of my best friends staying with me, I carried a lot of guilt knowing I influenced him to use heroin. He knew I was using because I didn't hide it. He knew I was selling it because people would come over all the time to buy it.

He asked about it, and curiosity got the better of him as well. My influence was toxic. I thought to myself, *You have to send him home. If you were a true friend, you would have never let him come out to visit, knowing that he would potentially end up wanting to try it.* From our past experiences of experimenting with drugs growing up, why wouldn't he want to try it? I knew better, but it still didn't prevent me from getting high with him.

The Meat and Potaotes

He was only supposed to come out to visit and see the city for a short time, and now, two months later, he was withdrawing from heroin. It wasn't too long after he got over being dope sick that he finally left, and I was glad. When he got on that bus I was so relieved, because I couldn't deal with the guilt any longer. One good thing that came out of him leaving was he never used heroin again.

Nothing about Pittsburgh felt right anymore. I remember when I first got there how excited I was about being in the city. How amazing the skyline and cultural food district was. Now that I'd experienced the darker side of it all, the only thing I could notice was the depressing smell of homelessness and piss as I walked downtown. I struggled with that feeling for the rest of my time in the city. I was so stubborn about admitting failure that I tried everything in my power to make college work. *How many times must I beat my head against the wall before accepting failure?*

I remember being downtown one day, walking around and exploring the city. It was a regular route of mine. Every so often I would pass by a particular church. I always admired the Gothic aesthetics of this historic structure. One random day, though, I decided to go in and take a look around. I was at an emotionally low point. All I remember was the overwhelming need to pray. I went to the altar, got down on my knees, and asked God to help get me through Pittsburgh.

A part of me was hoping to talk to a pastor, but no one came out. While I was in the church praying, I reflected back on my life and how my mom had done her best to keep us kids involved with the church. I got baptized when I was fifteen or so. One thing I never realized was that my relationship with God took work to understand. I never did that; I just thought I was saved and that life was good. As long as I could remember, I had always prayed, but I never took my faith seriously. It felt good to pray that day as I was looking for relief from the shame of my addiction.

I didn't find any long-term resolution from being in the church that day. Instead I went home and got high. I was depressed and lonely. Everything in my life felt like it was on the verge of completely falling apart. I was barely getting by with my grades in school. It felt like at any minute something bad was going to happen. After all, why wouldn't it? I wasn't living a normal life. Everything about my life was chaotic.

About two weeks later that same month, my fall quarter of school started. One night while walking to a bus stop after work, I was robbed by two people. I was hit in the face with a bat or a pipe of some kind, and they took my bookbag. My jaw was broken and my chin was fractured when I fell and landed on my face. I was knocked out cold. I didn't even see it coming when I got hit. It was so random and unexpected that I thought I had gotten hit by a cyclist or car from behind.

I blacked out for a moment but woke up and noticed my bookbag was gone, and I saw two shadowy figures running across the street. I started chasing the people who'd robbed me. My wallet and all my video footage that I was working on for graduation were in that bag. I managed to chase them about a block before they dropped my bag while cutting across a side street. I tried to yell at first, but I felt an unforgettable crunching pain on the side of my face. That's when I knew my jaw was broken.

I guess they thought there was more in my bag than books. My wallet was at the bottom of the bag, so they never got it. I found myself walking to the hospital in Oakland, Pennsylvania, the area where I worked. I knew I was in really bad shape. I did everything in my power to keep my mouth shut because the pain was excruciating. I knew the injury was bad because my mouth kept filling with blood. Once in the hospital, I passed out while waiting to be admitted. The next thing I knew, it was the next morning, and I was awakened by a nurse telling me that I was going in for emergency surgery.

I panicked because I had a video presentation due that morning in class. I convinced the hospital to discharge me. I went to the local pharmacy across from the bus stop on the way to class and got the prescription the hospital gave me for painkillers. I felt like shit and looked like death rolled over me. When I got to class my lab partner knew something was wrong and called me into the hall. My lab partner and the professor asked me what the hell was going on. I told both of them the whole story and explained that I was supposed to be in surgery.

They looked at me like I was crazy for skipping my surgery to come to class. I explained to them that I just didn't want to fail the presentation. The professor excused me with a makeup date, and my lab partner drove me back to the hospital. I think back now and realize how crazy my life was. Showing up to class with a broken jaw when I should have been in the hospital was insane. To me, it was merely an example of how out of control yet determined I was to follow through with my dream of being successful.

The surgery was performed, and I was in the hospital for five days. Instead of wiring my jaw shut, they put a plate on my jaw and a plate on my chin. I had a group of close friends from school at the time come to visit me at the hospital for a few hours. One of them told me to file a police report so I could apply for the victim-of-violence fund since I was a student from out of state.

That first night in the hospital was really bad for me, and the nurse came in and gave me Dilaudid a couple times through IV. During my years of using heroin, I would think back on it all, and I could remember the first feeling I had when the drug rushed into my system. Even when I was tired of being strung out, the familiar feeling would take me back to those nights in the hospital. It would only rekindle the obsessive compulsion to feel that high again. This vicious cycle was just starting, and I had no clue as to how big this monster would become in my life.

Later that week I spoke with a cop and a hospital representative from human resources. They helped me file for the medical relief fund. That surgery debt was eventually cleared, and the total amount including the stay was $70,000. After my surgery, it took me about three weeks before I was able to actually have a conversation and not be in a lot of pain. After three weeks I was able to present my video project. We received a fairly good grade for that final, but it definitely wasn't a fair trade.

While I was in the hospital I ended up losing my job. They fired me for a no-call no-show. I fought for the unemployment and eventually I ended up getting it. This only fueled my addiction during my last year in Pittsburgh. I had no structure in my life other than school, and even that wasn't going so well for me. I managed to graduate from the Art Institute of Pittsburgh in December 2005 but not without being high. During the ceremony I kept disappearing, going to the bathroom to use. Nobody knew it but I had close to $500-worth of dope on me that day.

The Meat and Potaotes

Shortly after graduating I moved to Cleveland with Amelia. We were living at her mom's house. At the time Mia was in rehab. My girlfriend and I continued to struggle with our addiction, and we were still driving to Pittsburgh every other day, sometimes every day depending on our usage. Six months after graduation we decided to split up. Our relationship had become so toxic that she began stealing from her family.

You're probably wondering why I didn't just get heroin from Cleveland if I was living in Cleveland. One, we didn't know anyone from Cleveland, and two, my connections allowed me prices we couldn't walk away from. It was cheaper and seemed safer to make the trip. The people I had been buying from for the past couple of years knew us, and it was just a better gamble.

In the end I didn't want to keep using, and it finally came to a point where I called my mom and asked her if she would come get me. I told my mom that my relationship with Amelia wasn't going well and that we hadn't been getting along for some time. I explained to her that ever since I graduated money wasn't good. I didn't have a car and I was living in the country. I needed help with getting back on my feet and asked her if she could come get me. She wasn't happy and there were more questions than answers at first. Eventually after some persuasion she agreed to come pick me up.

I explained to her that I had run out of money for college and wasn't able to continue with my education. I needed to continue with school for my bachelor's in audio, but Pittsburgh's Art Institute never started their audio program. The whole thing was a disaster. I told my mom everything except the truth. My mother was never on board with me leaving for Pittsburgh in the first place. My uncle Greg even came and talked to me before I left home, trying to get me to understand that people don't just go to an art institute without previous experience.

The reality was that I was strung out on dope now. I had no money and I had barely graduated college. My time at the Art Institute was nothing short of a failed attempt to make it on my own. Ultimately, I failed everything because of my drug usage. Yes, I did graduate, which says a lot, but had I put as much energy into my schooling as I did running around selling and using drugs, I believe I would have been very successful. Because I didn't truly apply myself 100 percent, I will never know.

Amelia's and my addiction was a financial disaster. We spent thousands of dollars in roughly three months. Ninety percent of it came from her. I was broke and had spent all of my money months earlier. I tried working for a short while, but even then I wasn't able to keep a job. My addiction interfered with my ability to function as a normal person.

At this time, my drug use went from every day of the week to several times a day. We were going through twenty-five bags each every two days. In the drug scene, ten bags are a bundle; fifty bags are a brick. We were using fifty bags between the two of us every two days. Two or three bags barely kept me from feeling weak and having cold sweats and the shits. My tolerance was through the roof. Remember, I was selling it, so everything I had been using up to now was free. Plus, don't forget I was selling other drugs as well, so I was always getting high from profits.

The day that my mom came to pick me up at Amelia's house in Cleveland, Amelia and I drove back to Pittsburgh for one last high together. We made it back right before my mom got to

Cleveland, but it was just a prime example of how desperate we had become in our addiction. Even though our relationship had started out with both of us genuinely in love with each other, it was quickly destroyed because of our drug use. In the end Amelia and I had only one thing in mind as a couple. Get high. We were driven by the obsessive compulsion to stay high. That drive from Cleveland to Pittsburgh was a perfect example of that selfish inner greed.

Seeing my mom for the first time in nearly six months was not a grand reunion. She was not happy to see me at all. As we drove away, I looked in the rearview mirror only to see Amelia standing at the edge of the driveway, slowly getting smaller as I drove further down the road. At this point in my life, the only thing that was more painful for me was when I got mugged while walking home from work.

I thought I knew what love was, and I truly believed that what I felt for the last three years was real. I realize now that codependency is what fueled our relationship. My thoughts and feelings were clouded by the dope. The truth was right in front of me that day. The realization of the withdrawals was sure to come in the next twenty-four hours. I was hurting inside because I knew that this chapter of my life was over for good. I briefly reflected on how many relationships had been torn during my time in Pittsburgh. I thought about how things could have been different. My first roommates were all good people, but we had a falling out over the relationship I was in. Now, even that relationship was over.

Obviously, I made the wrong decisions, and I couldn't see it at the time, even though other contributing factors drove my roommates and me apart. It was because of the girl I was dating. They didn't agree with the choices I was making. I'm not sure if they knew I was using heroin because it was never brought up, but a part of me wished I had talked about it. My roommates were good friends. We had a lot of great memories in the beginning. In the end, heroin ruined everything during my time in Pittsburgh. It turned into a huge disaster.

The two-hour car ride home was mostly filled with me answering questions about the lies I had been living. I kept finding ways to spin more lies into a believable story. I was trying to convince my mom and family back home that things were better than they actually were. After three and a half years of being away from home, my family still didn't know about my heroin addiction. I had never felt so low and consumed with negative self-talk. It felt so good to feel bad for myself, because that's how my addiction wanted me to live my life—miserable. While using in Pittsburgh when I began to have fear or concerns, I would just get high to escape it. If I was mad, I would use, and if I began to have doubts within myself, I would use.

This toxic criticism was fueling the pain and strangely motivating me as well. It's hard to explain. Despite the overwhelming reminder of how much of a failure I had become, deep down I knew that I was destined for so much more in life. I just couldn't put my finger on what that purpose truly was.

I finally nodded off for about an hour before we made it back home. When we got to the house it was an immediate reminder of my past and what was left behind years ago. I was different now. Things weren't perceived through the innocent perspective that once ran around this house. Everything seemed smaller and simpler. I was back to the place I once so desperately wanted to leave. I felt sad and ashamed and had an overwhelming sense to leave again. But what was I running from?

This place had me feeling trapped. It was the primary reason I left in the first place. This town seemed like it wasn't big enough for me anymore. Everything I once knew wasn't the same. Everyone was older, and the streets where I once rode my bike were colder and felt darker. I felt dirty and sick. I thought to myself, *You're a fucking loser.* I started getting depressed. I started getting cold chills. I wanted to run, but I also wanted to find a place to curl up in a ball and hide. Something was off. Why was I feeling like I couldn't explain what I was feeling? I wanted to get high, and I had no dope. The last time I had gotten high was that afternoon, and that's when it hit me. That voice hit me like a brick wall. *You'll know when you're sick.* I was reminded of a conversation I thought I would never recall. Out of all the experiences in life that I had to be reminded of, I remembered the conversation I had with a stranger while at a party. I was dope sick.

Heroin

Why have I done this to myself?
Why did I choose to push away my help?
This love in my blood was a kiss in the wind,
a demon that bit me and left me with nothing.
Forgive me for what's been done, I need your love.
A plume in the poison only made me numb.
The cloud I was on was nothing close to fun.
The needle in my hand was a loaded gun.
You say that you want, even though they're all lies.
Who would have thought I'd walk away from this alive?
With broken skin these scars were my pride.
I accepted my fate and continued to get high.
In my heart I wanted to get clean.
Odds stacked against me seemed like a never-ending dream.
This demon takes your soul and leaves you cold.
It robs you of your purpose and steals your goals!

2.
AND SO IT BEGINS!

The next twenty-four hours were rough. I was depressed, and I was experiencing hot flashes and cold sweats. My body ached, and I had diarrhea. It was worse than having the flu. I couldn't sleep for most of the next week, and I spent my nights smoking weed and drinking with the few friends who were still in town. One of my closest friends as a kid was Big Country. He lived only a few houses down on the same street as me. I first met Big Country when I moved to Ohio from Texas.

He was one of the first kids to ask me to hang out with him after school in the sixth grade. We would ride bikes in the woods where there were ramps and dirt trails. This was where all the kids occasionally hung out and rode their bikes. As kids, we would do our paper routes on Saturdays together, go to the skating rink, and even fish at the reservoirs on the weekends. Growing up and having a paper route was common in my town. It wasn't something that all the kids my age had, but I thought it was cool being trusted with a paper route. Plus, the money was a reward. As we got older, the paper routes faded, and eventually sports became the focus. I went to the YMCA and was on the swimming team. I also played soccer and played the trumpet in the concert band and marching band.

We were typical small-town boys. Big Country played baseball growing up and naturally went on to play football as an offensive and defensive tackle. He got his nickname because of how big he was. Our freshman year, he was six feet tall and 230 pounds. Blond hair, blue eyes—typical German. He had tree trunks for forearms, but his strength was often underestimated because he was always cracking jokes and was very friendly. Being around Big Country, I knew I was always in good company.

Our families were proud as we excelled in our hobbies. In baseball, he was known as a home run hitter. During our freshman year, the football team went on to win the championship for our high school division. He and everyone on the team earned themselves championship rings that year. I, on the other hand, earned my varsity letter in soccer as a freshman. The team and I were undefeated in soccer and won our championship that year. These were very momentous achievements for us and our community at the time.

Growing up, Big Country seemed to have no fear and was always up for a challenge. He knew everyone and was a brother from another mother to me. We both called each other's mom "Mom." We could come over and eat at one another's house anytime, no questions asked. Everything seemed simpler back then. Early on in high school, everything changed, though. We began to make bad choices from the unhealthy peer pressure that was around us. Every town has its own set of issues. My town was known for drugs and alcohol.

As a sophomore, I began experimenting with alcohol and smoking weed. Although years have gone by since the passing of Big Country's brother Cody, one thing was for certain: He was still down to hang out. Even though he was still living at home with his parents, it was comforting to be welcomed back by a supportive/familiar face. As I approached his house for the first time in years, he was outside on a ladder. He was scraping the old paint off the house, prepping it for new paint. We spent the next few days catching up, sharing stories, smoking weed, and drinking. I even helped him paint his parents' house.

It was almost like nothing had changed other than the day's date and our age. Eventually, the topic of my heroin addiction was brought up. We talked about what it was like living in Pittsburgh. He already knew I was using heroin. He came to Pittsburgh and visited me one random weekend after I had lived out there for about two years. He never judged me, though. Instead, he got high with me and admitted to using OxyContin back home. Turns out OxyContin and heroin use were more common back home than I had expected.

After talking about it, I wanted to get high again. Yet a part of me had an aversion to the idea. When I began to think of how miserable those last few days were from detoxing, it quickly reminded me of how overwhelmingly fucked up I still was emotionally. Deep down, I knew using heroin again was going to be like opening Pandora's box. Deep inside, I didn't care. I was miserable, and in a sick, twisted way, I was craving the pain.

Big Country and his family were still grieving from the loss of their loved one, Cody, who had passed away in 2001. It was still fresh in everyone's mind, including mine. Big Country had his own set of issues. He was trying to suppress the pain, and so he and I together were only going to increase the possibility of using again. I understood the family's pain because I felt it too. The old saying "misery loves company" held true for both of us. Deep down inside, we were miserable.

I've always carried a personal burden knowing my father was never around. It was just me, my mother, sister, and brother. My mom's immediate family was from Ohio. It was only natural that she would return there to raise her children once Texas was no longer an option. My mother did everything she could to raise us kids right. Bringing us to a small town made more sense. I was the oldest of the children. All of my siblings were four years apart. I was the only child of my father, and my brother and sister never really knew their dad either. My mother left their father at an age that made it hard for them to remember specifics like I did. Their dad was a physically and emotionally abusive alcoholic. I never really shared my burdens with any of my friends growing up. I felt embarrassed and ashamed of it. I just wanted to grow up and try to forget it.

Growing up and seeing other kids with their mother and father made me reflect on a deeper level. I felt most of the kids in my town would never be able to identify with me. As I got older, and I realized the other kids were drinking and smoking, it made it easier to fit in. I saw it as a commonality that we all shared. I was just looking for a deeper sense of acceptance. This was a way to separate how differently I viewed myself from the rest of the kids when I was younger.

Being one of the last people to see Cody before he passed away has stuck with me over the years. He was home from school on medical leave from a football injury. His grandpa was a successful retired doctor who had recently passed away. When the family sold the house, a lot of his old belongings, including his medical bags, were moved into their home.

In 2001, while home alone, Cody went through those belongings, found a vial of pills, and started taking them. A group of our friends would hang out after school and smoke weed and party. On a particular day in March, Cody was handing out the pills and telling everyone to take a few. He gave me about five or six tablets. I asked him what they were, and that's when he said it was morphine. I took a couple, but I didn't feel confident in taking all of them. By the end of the afternoon, we left and went to another friend's house. That's about the time I started to feel sick. I told Cody I was about to leave and asked him if he wanted to go home. Cody said, "Let me call home. If my dad's there, I'm staying here until later."

When he called home, his father answered the phone and started yelling at him. You could hear him screaming, and I knew he was in trouble. So, he said he wasn't going home. Cody asked me if I wanted the empty vial. I got it because it looked cool. I thought maybe I could use it for something later. When I got home, I fell asleep only to wake up later that night sick because of the pills. The next morning, my sister called home from school. She was crying, telling me Cody was dead.

It was a tragic situation, and we were all close. Me and Big Country were in the same grade. My sister and Cody were in the same grade, and my brother and Ryan (Big Country and Cody's little brother) were in the same grade. I couldn't believe what I was hearing at first, so I called Big Country's house. That's when I found out it was true. There was a conviction in me to do the right thing by explaining to the family exactly what had happened.

I walked down to their house and gave the parents the vial. Cody's immediate family was there in the kitchen, sitting around the table, grieving. They were consoling Cody's parents. I pulled the vial out of my pocket and put it on the table. Cody's family members looked at each other as if they were surprised to see it, yet aware of where it came from. The reaction was disbelief and shock as I told them everything.

I explained how the previous day Cody got to the house where he died. I remember feeling awkward and ashamed as I was describing to the family his last hours alive. I explained to them that I was starting to feel sick and told Cody I was going to leave. I told them I offered him a ride home, but he stayed because he knew he would be in trouble when he went home. Everything I told Cody's family was explained word for word in the police report I had to file. It was by far the hardest thing I had ever experienced while growing up. In the end, Cody's death was ruled an accidental overdose.

During the next few days or so after Cody's death, I called Big Country's house and spoke with his parents. His father asked me if I would be a pallbearer. Of course, I accepted. After I got off the phone with them, I started crying again because a part of me still felt responsible. I felt like I should have done more, even though there was nothing I could have done differently. Had I not been there, I would have never known about the pills; however, the outcome would still have been the same. Cody still would have taken the pills. The only difference would have been that I wouldn't have taken the pills.

And So It Begins!

That day of the procession was a moment in my life I will never forget. It was spring, and during his burial, it began to snow—the largest snowflakes you could imagine. There was no wind; it felt supernatural to me, and I looked at it as symbolic. As I drove away after the ceremony, I was accompanied by a few friends. The radio played "Tuesday's Gone" and "Free Bird" by Lynyrd Skynyrd back-to-back. We were all smoking weed and drinking when I noticed the songs. I'm not sure if any of the other guys picked up on it, but those songs were exactly who Cody was.

The oversized snowflakes on a spring day and the music on the radio were the epitome of who Cody was. I felt that in some kind of way, he was speaking to us. He was fascinated with the '60s and '70s. He loved Jimi Hendrix, Lynyrd Skynyrd, and similar music from that era. Cody's passing changed me as much as it changed his whole family. Even the nostalgia that our small town once had made life emotionally harder. It brought a cloud over the once-sunny innocence that our water-tower town had when I was growing up.

Over the years, I would frequently visit the family plot. A loss like that never leaves your soul. You're burdened with it constantly. At times, it's hard to think past the passing of that loved one. The shame, the sorrow, the questions of *what if* and *why*. They rob you of your peace, and you find yourself doing whatever it takes to bury that pain. A lot of times, you just say, "Fuck it," and do the first thing that comes to mind. For me and I'm sure his family, it was getting high to pass the time and suppress the pain. Distraction is the devil's best gimmick when it comes to stealing your purpose. The next thing you know, you look back and years have gone by. The town has changed, and people are older. The trees get bigger, and the locusts return at the end of summer every year. However, the headstone remains the same: frozen in time.

There I was, back in my hometown, faced with my past and trying to pick up the pieces to my life. As time went on, I found myself a decent factory job with good insurance. Before I knew it, I had been home a year without using heroin, even though I was still going to the bars, using cocaine, smoking weed, and staying up all night partying in the clubs. After my grandfather died, that's when I went off the deep end with using heroin again. A few guys at work were into heroin, and they knew of my past. They offered an invitation from time to time, and finally, I took it.

They paid for the gas, and they got me high for free; all I did was drive. So thoughtful, right? Yeah, that's how it goes. Birds of a feather flock together. They all move and think alike. That night turned into more than just a dope run. It turned into a freaking curse for me, because the dope boy in the city gave me his phone number. I went back the following week after I got paid. You think I would have learned my lesson after all the pain from the past, right? Well, nothing had changed in my life up to this point. I was still partying, and I wasn't working on myself. I wasn't trying to have a deeper understanding of why I was so obsessed with running from my problems. I wasn't trying to evaluate my toxic behaviors. I was consumed with the distractions that felt most comfortable. Those thoughts were followed by the ever-recurring negative self-talk that nagged me about my past.

Of course, I wanted more out of life. I just couldn't figure out how to tap into changing it. When I went to see the dope dealer by myself, I got more than I had anticipated. It was three times as much. The first thing I asked was, "Is this fifty-dollars worth?" I realized I could sell half and get my money back. Just like that, I was back where I left off with selling so that I could use heroin for free.

One thing led to another, and before I knew it, one by one, people were asking me for dope. Eventually, I was selling enough dope that I didn't have to cash my work checks on Fridays. Around that same time I had started spending time with a girl, Julia. I met her while working at the factory. It wasn't long after we started spending more time together that she found out I was selling heroin. I thought to myself that I really should keep my distance from her because of my addiction. Her persistence and my people-pleasing led to us being more than just friends. We knew a lot of the same people, and by this time, there were more people in the surrounding area using heroin than I ever would have guessed. By the time we started dating, I had already started shooting up heroin. I still remember the first time I used a needle. That day has been embedded in me like a red wine stain on a white carpet.

Big Country was with me, and the guy who taught us the ins and outs went by the nickname "the Old Man." He gave us both a stark warning that day as he held a lighter under the spoon. As he proceeded to teach us how to use a needle, he said, "If you want to be miserable, alone, and have nothing in life, keep doing this and it will give you everything you're looking for." I took that warning with a grain of salt as Big Country chuckled.

The place where we used a needle for the first time was known as the Crack Mansion. I met the Old Man and learned about the mansion from selling dope. It was a dilapidated apartment complex that looked like a mansion from the outside. The building was a white three-story complex that had chipped paint all over the outside. As you entered through the front door, the wood trim and handrails revealed their past elegance. The wallpaper and carpet also told a story of an era frozen in time. Now it was all worn down from years of neglect and foot traffic. From the outside looking up at the building, you could see that at one point in history, this place stood with grace. Over the decades, it had lost its facade. For me, it now had a dark cloud hovering over top of it that vibrated with negative energy. It was created from the drug deals and drug use that had overcome the place. Nonetheless, it has been marked in my timeline of memories that were fueled by my addiction.

At this point, I had been selling and using drugs for close to six months. I had more money than I initially intended. In the beginning, I was just looking to sell so I could get high for free. Why would I have an incentive to stop using it if it was free? From the beginning, my relationship with Julia was toxic. She was a single mother, and her son was caught right in the middle of all her attempts at trying to settle down. Given my selfishness of just wanting to get high, I should never have gotten involved with her. Instead, I had now entangled her and her son into this web of destruction. When I moved in with her, Julia was already snorting heroin with me. It wasn't long after that that she found the needles in my car. That's about the time she started shooting heroin. My relationship with her lasted for about two or so years, and during that time, she was helping me sell dope.

The most tragic thing about the relationship was that there was a child involved. We were constantly arguing about dope and breaking up. I would leave and then come back. My biggest regret with that relationship was knowing that a child was exposed to our addiction and that I was the root cause of her addiction. Even though it was her choice to use heroin, I would have rather it been someone else who exposed her to it than me. Even to this day, as I write this, it's hard admitting the fact that I played a major role in so many people's exposure to heroin. As I write this, knowing what I did, I would want justice. I would want to beat my ass. As a father now, I would want retribution for exposing my child to this evil. Sure, it's anger and pride and ego, but it's also a matter of right from wrong. I have no idea where Julia is today, and I have no idea how this child's life has turned out. I've prayed for both of them over the years, and I truly hope that their lives are better now.

Words can't undo what was done, and I'm the one who has to live with those burdens. As much as I tried to distance myself from Julia early on, I tried even harder to keep my mother, sister, and family shielded from what I was doing. Deep inside, I knew they knew something wasn't right. There were many times when we wound up in heated discussions over my behavior. It would be followed by suspicions of drug use, even though no one could prove it. I was back living with my mother again, and eventually I got another job. By this time, my drug use had become so bad that I was shooting several times a day. I remember one early morning, I was getting ready for work, and I was downstairs in the kitchen being loud. My sister came down and started arguing with me.

She picked up an antique crystal candy jar and threatened to hit me with it. I told her if she hit me with it, it would be the last thing she ever did. I told her I would kill her and then kill myself because I didn't care anymore. That moment changed everything between my sister and me for years to come. I instantly regretted what I said, and the look on her face was one of shock, like she had just been handed terrifying news. You could see the hurt in her eyes.

The car ride to work with my mom that morning was so depressing. She was listening to Pastor James McDonald on the radio. To be honest, I don't even remember the message. I was consumed with negative self-talk and distracted with wanting to get high before work started.

It wasn't too much longer after that incident that I ended up quitting that job for the same reasons again. The job was interfering with my drug usage. Since moving home from Pittsburgh, my drug usage had created more problems for me than ever before. All my decision-making in the previous few years had been based on having to get high so that I wasn't dope sick. Turned out the only thing I was good at was making bad decisions.

It was from this chapter in my life that "Car Ride of Sorrow" was written. I was in prison when I wrote this poem. It was because of my journaling that I was able to reflect on this incident in my life and begin to process how my addiction affected my family.

Car Ride of Sorrow

I scream inside my mind with sorrow,
and my soul is pouring tears.
I'm looking out the window, ashamed and filled with fear.
Just tell her your pain, regardless of the shame.
It's no longer an issue about causing her pain.

My sick, pale skin with dark circles around my eyes told a story
that I've been so desperate to hide.
For far too long, I've barely gotten by, and here I sit,
consumed with lies.
My arms bear the scars from the beast called disease;
My eyes whimper with despair from tears of defeat.
I'm so tired of this ride! What have I done?
Just tell her the truth, just tell her for once.
My fear is that I'll hurt her, pain I'm afraid to bear.
After all, this isn't the first time I've succumbed to this affair.
Mother, I'm truly sorry, I'm crying from inside.
In the end, only tears were shed during this sorrowful car ride.

Selling heroin was the only thing I knew I could do to support my drug habit. What a vicious cycle I'd been living in. People would pay me to drive and pick up dope because I had the connections. My little side hustle worked out for the most part because I was able to get it cheaper than the average person who was using it. I'd been going to the same dealer for a couple of years now, so it worked in my favor.

Things were starting to change in my community due to the overwhelming presence of heroin. Stress was mounting, and it seemed like every week, I was learning about a fatal overdose within the surrounding counties. Until now, it wasn't anyone I knew. Drug busts were becoming more and more common, and theft was becoming more of a problem. I never robbed homes out of desperation for more dope. I used my networking skills to collect people's money. People trusted me. It's a disgusting way to look at it. However, at the time, I justified it as being okay. I would tell myself, *at least they're not getting ripped off*, or *at least I know what I'm getting is good*. It eventually got to the point that the dope dealers trusted me enough to give me heroin for free up front. In return, I would bring the money back and get more.

There were plenty of times people would call me a couple of days after coming home from detox or rehab, looking to get high. I wouldn't help them because I so desperately dreamed of being in their situation, as if somehow it would mean a better life for me. I would tell them, "It's not worth it. You're not missing anything. You have a fresh start, and I'm not selling it to you." I wanted to stop, but I couldn't. I didn't have insurance or the money for rehab. The facilities charged exorbitant amounts of money just to house you for detox. Most of the time, it led to disagreements and even arguments with them because I wouldn't sell dope to them after they got out of rehab, but that's just how I felt about the matter.

On the other hand, some people who called me were so sick that I felt I had no choice but to help them get high. I knew how bad it was to be dope sick. I was using a few hundred dollars of dope a day, and I was selling around two ounces or more. In the end, Big Country and I were even smoking crack with his parents. Everyone knew Big Country's dad smoked, but it really got bad years later. When I came home from Pittsburgh, it was more of an openly talked-about thing. Even though it was no secret that Big Country and Ryan were smoking with their parents, I really wasn't part of that equation until right before prison. We had been through so much over the years that I could write another chapter on our experiences growing up as kids.

Right before prison something occurred that will always remain one of my "what the fuck" stories. It happened like this. It was winter, and Big Country drove me back to the city amid a level-two snowstorm. There was snow and ice on the highways, and he asked if it was safe to put the car in cruise control. Sixty to sixty-five miles an hour on cruise control? "I don't know," I replied. Five minutes later, out of nowhere, the car started slipping. He cut the steering wheel hard left and the car began to spin out of control. We slid across two lanes of highway sideways and hit the side of the snow-filled grass median. Big Country slammed on the gas, and we did another 180. He corrected the car, and we were back to driving like nothing happened.

We were both shaken up, thinking, *What the fuck just happened?* I had drugs on me. I had a digital scale to weigh the heroin, and I had needles and several thousand dollars in cash. We pulled off at the next rest stop. We got out to check the car, and there wasn't a scratch on the car. We got back in the car, and as we were getting back on the highway, a state highway patrol car drove by. You can't make this stuff up.

The summer leading up to my arrest in July 2011, on my birthday, I remember doing some serious soul-searching. I thought about the fact that I was now thirty years old. I was on my way to the city again to buy more dope. I so desperately wanted a better life. I wanted to change, but I was also cornered by the fact that I was addicted to heroin. A vicious revolving door of constant reminders.

I remember telling myself on the way up to the city, "Today is the last day I'm going to use. I'm done." This wasn't the first time I told myself this mantra, though. That same day, on our way back home, Big Country and I passed a sheriff on the country road. It wasn't a quarter mile down when the sheriff pulled a U-turn. We had both been through this routine before and knew that the sheriff was going to attempt to pull us over.

I had scales and dope on me, and we both had needles. I quickly hid everything, and we pulled into a country-house driveway, attempting to make it look like we lived there. The sheriff kept on driving by. In my mind, I believe that we had narrowly escaped being pulled over and searched. We waited five minutes or so, discussing what our story was going to be if we did end up getting pulled over. We got back on the road going the opposite direction, thinking we could take a different route back into town. It wasn't a mile down another road that the sheriff came flying up behind us again. We were pulled over this time, and both of us were searched, including the vehicle. We were asked what we were up to and why we had attempted to avoid being pulled over. Our stories matched that it was my birthday, and we went to eat in the city. We missed our road coming home and were just turning around.

The sheriff ended up letting us go, but what the sheriff said next is what got my attention. He didn't say anything else to Big Country, and instead he said, "You take care of yourself, Edward, and have a happy birthday." I found it strange at the time, but I also just wanted to get the hell home. Why did he say that, though? I felt it was sarcasm, as if there was more to his birthday wish. Nonetheless, I was eager to get off the road. These trips were beginning to become more and more stressful, and I just wished it would all end.

And So It Begins!

A month later, in August, just when I thought my addiction couldn't make me feel any lower, my brother had his second daughter. I went to visit them in the hospital, and they asked if I wanted to hold my niece for the first time. I told them no. I didn't hold her because I was dope sick and I didn't want to touch her. I felt dirty and toxic and thought that by holding her, I would make her sick.

That same week, I remember lying in bed one day, depressed, sick, and just tired of getting high. I had track marks on the inside of both my arms that ran from my wrists to my elbows. I had been shooting up several times a day for the last few years. I was thirty years old, living with my mom, no job, no car—a complete waste of life at this point. It had now been over five years since I moved home from college. I'd been through multiple jobs and another toxic relationship with nothing to show for any of it. Flipping channels on TV, I recall coming across Pastor Joel Osteen's channel. I began praying with him about forgiveness.

On this day, I prayed to God. For the first time in my life, I just told God everything. It's strange to say, but there was a revelation that I experienced at that moment. This time was different than any other time I had prayed before. For the first time in my life, I truly understood how powerless I was. Until then, I had never submitted to the fact that I wasn't in control. I fought for so long inside my mind, thinking I could fix the problems I had created.

Now I realized that my battle was a supernatural and spiritual one. The revelation I had was based on the nature of my relationship with God. It was that God is the parent who knows his child has done wrong. Your father loves you with all his heart, and he is hurt that you haven't come clean with him. Yet he is still going to clothe you, feed you, care for you, and love you. Outside of those circumstances, he is just waiting for you to come clean to him about everything you've done wrong. Well, that's how it felt for me when I started talking to God. I told God everything: my fears, my bad choices, and the life I was living.

I told God, "I know that You have something great for me in life, but I can't see it." The more I prayed, the harder I gripped my hands. I eventually got to the point where I was on my knees, white-knuckled, praying, just asking God to help me find a way out. I asked God to take me or leave me. I just wanted this nightmare to end.

I kid you not, for a moment, all that pain was gone. I didn't have anxiety. I didn't have fear. I felt relieved, as if the weight had been lifted at that moment. The difference between praying to God this time versus all the other times was that this time, I wasn't just trying to feel better in the moment. I truly wanted to change.

Then the phone rang. A rush of excitement and joy filled my body that could only be described as relief. I was hoping it was someone with money who wanted to buy dope. I needed to get high. My dysfunctional belief system had me believing that God was helping me with another opportunity to get high so that I would stop withdrawing. I completely forgot about the one-on-one I just had with God.

Soon after that phone call ended, I was dressed and outside, waiting to be picked up. My heroin use didn't stop until a month later, on September 22, 2011. By this time, I had been using heroin for over eight years in total. On this one particular day in

And So It Begins!

September, I took a ride to the city with someone I had been getting dope with for a couple of years. I was set to make some money along with extra heroin as profit. Big Country's birthday was that weekend, and so he and I had plans to get high. I got the dope, and we made it back to town. I called and told him to meet me at my mom's house. On the drive through town, we got pulled over.

It happened so fast that we were blocked off in traffic by other vehicles from the front and the back. I thought we were getting in a car accident until several agents with DEA vests jumped out of all the vehicles. I panicked and locked the doors. The cops had their guns drawn, screaming through the glass to get out of the car. The guy who drove me wouldn't even make eye contact with me. He just kept saying, "I'm sorry, I'm sorry, man, my kid, I didn't have any other choice." I knew I had been set up. Amid all the chaos, I knew it was finally over. I yelled, "You have no idea what you have just done, this is bigger than you or me!" That's when everything went quiet, and all I could do was remember praying a month back, asking God for help.

God spoke to me in the car that day. He told me, "You did this to yourself. I will never leave you, and I have plans for you far greater than you could ever imagine. However, you must change your life." I told the driver, "You know what, I wish you the best in life. You saved my life, man." He turned his head so fast and looked at me like he saw a ghost. I told him I was going to change my life, and that's when I opened the car door. The DEA agent snatched me out of the car and threw me to the ground. The agent had his knee on my back and had his forearm on the back of my neck. He cuffed me and pulled me up.

As I got up, I made eye contact with another arresting officer. He called me by my name with a tone of surprise. It was a guy I had graduated from high school with. By the look on his face, he was stunned. He said, "What the hell is going on?" I said, "I don't know what to say. I'm in bad shape and I need help." I was taken to jail and booked. That's when the detectives came in and told me they had been watching me for a month. They told me I was being charged with felony possession and trafficking heroin. That's when they showed me a bunch of pictures of people I had been getting high with over the past few years, and that's when I told them I wanted a lawyer present.

I couldn't even hold my head up. I was so ashamed and shocked at everything that had just happened. I asked to make my one phone call during processing, and I called my mom. I told her I had been arrested and that I wouldn't be coming home. She asked why, and I told her it was for heroin trafficking. You could hear her on the phone screaming at me. I could hear my sister in the background. "Ha-ha, it serves you right!" I couldn't stay on the phone any longer and bear hearing the disappointment in my mother's voice.

I just wanted to sleep and forget about it. For the first twenty-four hours, that's exactly what I did: I slept the heroin off. The next day, I was transferred to the county, already feeling the heroin withdrawals. I was put on medical observation for detox. While I was in that cell, I tossed and turned so much, I rubbed my sides raw. I didn't eat for days and could barely keep any liquids down. At six-foot-three, I weighed 150 pounds at the time of booking. At some point during my detox, I remember someone coming in and putting blankets on me.

The blankets were warm as if they had just come out of the dryer. It felt so good on my aching body. It was amazing how much that helped me. Eventually, I started to come around to feeling better and found out I was being moved from detox to the general population. I asked if they knew who had given me the warm blankets. The guard looked at me with confusion and said, "I'm on the night shift and I watched you all week. We almost took you to the hospital because we've never seen anyone come in as sick as you. I can assure you no one gave you warm blankets."

To this day, I can't explain it because I know I was given warm blankets. I heard the cell door open. I was so weak I couldn't even roll over to see anyone, but I know I was given warm blankets. I asked what day it was, and they told me Friday. I said, "Friday?" The guard said, "Yeah, you've been in detox for a week." I seriously thought it was only three days—that's how out of it I was. At this point, I just wanted to take a hot shower and use the phone. I hadn't talked to my mom for a week, and I knew she was worried.

3.

The Awakening

I was uncertain about what to expect going into the general population, but I had no choice in the matter. I was going in regardless. At this point, I just wanted a shower and a phone call. I made my bed and took my shower. It was the first shower I had in a week, and honestly, the hot water gave me relief. While taking my shower, I thought about how I was clean for the first time since I was fifteen. No drugs or alcohol, and I was proud of it. I used that as my focus.

My senses were still very off, though. Everything seemed extremely loud. The lights were bright, and I still didn't have a big appetite. But it sure felt good to take that shower. As I walked over to the pay phones, there were a few guys playing cards at one of the tables, and one of them asked me if I wanted to play a hand. I said no, maybe later; I needed to make a phone call. That's when the guy asked me, "Aren't you the guy that was in the paper?" I replied, "I don't know. It depends on what paper."

Come to find out, I was on the front page of the local paper a few days back. I followed the guy to his bed to get the paper, and when he gave it to me, he also said he had an extra Bible if I wanted it. I didn't even hesitate. I said yes. That defining moment changed the entire course of my incarceration. That evening, I was finally able to get a hold of my mom, and it felt longer than a week had passed since I had heard her voice. I missed my mom so much, and I just wanted to fast-forward this whole situation and come home.

She was crying, and it was hard to find the courage to stay on the phone with her. I started crying because I was still overwhelmed with emotions. I knew I was going to prison, and even though it was county jail, I was still incarcerated. I knew I wasn't coming home anytime soon. There was no getting out of this until it was time for court. I'd been running for far too long, and all I could think about was the fact that I had done this to myself.

For once in my life, I couldn't blame anyone, anyplace, or anything for my problems. I had to face the cold, harsh reality myself. My fifteen-minute phone call felt like two minutes. As I answered all my mom's questions and finally told her the truth about my drug usage, the time went by so quickly. She wanted to know if I had heard from a lawyer yet and when I was going to court—all of which I had no answers to. She was truly in shambles over the fact that I was not only using heroin but that I was selling it. I told her that as soon as I heard from my lawyer, I would call her and let her know what I knew.

As time went by, I continued to count the days of clean time I had. One week turned into two, and next thing I knew, I hit thirty days. I was finally served my indictment papers and found out I was being charged with seven felonies—five for trafficking and two for possession. I eventually made it to court and requested a court-appointed attorney. I didn't have any money, and there was nothing I could do. I had to wait for the court to appoint one. This legal process was new to me. I'd never really been in any kind of real trouble before. Time moved slowly as I awaited more information.

A day felt like a week at first. I got into a routine and started to do push-ups and pull-ups to help pass the time. Let's be clear, though. After all those years of drugs and alcohol, I couldn't do ten push-ups, let alone one pull-up. I didn't give up, though. It felt refreshing having this determination to start getting myself in shape. It took about a week before my mom gave me some money, which we called "books" in jail and in prison. The jails and prisons allow you to have money saved in the system if your family or loved ones can afford to send you money. You can buy things like hygiene products, food and snacks, and notepads, pencils, and envelopes if you want or need to write.

In the beginning, I didn't know how to start with my writing, so I started writing poems. Ever since my years of taking acid and experimenting with other hallucinogens, I had had an urge to put something on paper. I just didn't know where to start. Turns out being in jail gives you plenty of time to sort things out. I was writing in an attempt to find healing. I needed a distraction, but also a way to clear my mind.

It took about a month or so before my lawyer finally received my discovery packet. A discovery packet is every bit of information documented during an investigation to ensure that there was indeed enough evidence to charge someone with a crime. I'm not a lawyer, so this is just my general explanation. My lawyer and I spent several months combing through all the material.

I realized early on that I had a good court-appointed attorney. He seemed genuinely concerned for me and listened to me as I pleaded that I needed help. By help, I mean some kind of rehabilitation. I explained to him the fact that I was merely facilitating an active drug addiction. He helped me put together a list of evidence that didn't add up in regards to the case. There were dates and times, and locations that I was not a part of. What was surprising about the evidence was the pictures. The detectives had pictures of me getting out of vehicles at gas stations and my house. They even had pictures of me mowing my yard and meeting the informant in my driveway. Those pictures along with the audio recordings were damning.

The most interesting part of the discovery was the typed-up conversations that were recorded from a wiretap during my investigation. I found out that one of the dope dealers had turned informant to get out of his arrest. It was right there in black and white. He stated, and I quote, "If you want me to cooperate, you're going to have to keep me in jail for a few days or else my people will know I am cooperating." At this point, I didn't know what the heck was going on. I asked my lawyer how much time he thought I might be looking at. He closed his laptop and looked me in the eyes and said, "I'm going to be honest with you. The prosecuting attorney is recommending eleven years." My lawyer then told me that because I had never been in trouble, he thought he could get it lowered with the possibility of an early release if I managed to stay out of trouble. I thought to myself, *What a heck of a way to get in trouble for the first time.* While going back to the dorm that afternoon, I was sick to my stomach over the eleven-year offer. I didn't even want to tell my mom, and at first,

I wanted to wait until I heard back from my lawyer with a better offer. Three weeks went by before my lawyer came back with an offer from the prosecutor recommending eight years. With all this to be considered, I told my lawyer I shouldn't have to serve more than three years. I'd never been in trouble. I wouldn't even be in this situation if I had never used heroin.

In the back of my mind, though, I thought to myself that the best thing I had to look forward to out of all this was that I was going to be clean when I came home. Yet eight years still felt extreme. I asked my lawyer to tell the prosecutor no. My lawyer told me the best we could do at this point was wait. He told me he would see what he could do next time he met with them. Before I left, my lawyer advised me by saying, "You don't get many more options."

That night when I got back to the dorm, I heard a familiar voice call out my name. I looked over toward the phone area, and it was Big Country. I said, "You have to be freaking kidding me." I was so happy to see him. A feeling of joy came over me that I didn't think I would ever experience while in jail. We grabbed each other's hands, which was then met with a solid hug and a pat on the back. Turns out he had a civil protection order filed on him by his dad. A civil protection order restrains someone from contacting or approaching another person, usually regarding harassment, domestic violence, or stalking.

In his case the cops were called on him for trespassing. The whole thing started years earlier after they got into an altercation over drugs and money. The CPO was never lifted. While Big Country was at his parents' house getting a few things, his dad called the cops, and now he was in jail.

We had a lot of catching up to do. Most importantly, he wasn't strung out on heroin anymore. I told him everything about my case, and from what he was explaining, everyone around town knew who told on me. Apparently, the guy had set up other people after me. Big Country told me he had been clean for about a month. I was happy to see him clean, even though we were in jail. The whole experience was weird because I just couldn't believe we were in county jail together.

What are the odds that with everything happening in my life, my friend was here with me before I went to prison? I told him everything I was doing to better myself and that I had every intention to make the best of this unfortunate situation. He was happy for me and told me he was proud of me for how I was handling my circumstances. Christmas came, and the next thing I knew, 2012 was here. During the first business week of the new year, my lawyer came to visit and told me the prosecutor was offering seven years, eleven months. This is where it gets technical, so bear with me, because there are specifics as to why I took this offer.

At the time that I was sentenced, in the state of Ohio, if you were sentenced to five years, you would have had to do the whole five. The same came with a ten-year sentence. However, in my case, some of my charges were run together, with three years made mandatory. After the mandatory three years, that left me with four years, eleven months of non-mandatory time. One month. One month was the only thing that separated me from doing eight years in the state penitentiary. When my lawyer explained it to me, I told him I would agree to that. I knew I could do that. I thought about how long I had struggled with heroin and how fucked my life was. This was going to go by fast, in my opinion. My twenties had been a waste and a blur, if I'm being honest with you.

I knew my time here in the county jail was coming to an end. I wanted to go back to the dorm and call my mom and explain everything to her. I was relieved to finally have a bit of clarity as I waited to go before the judge. The only caveat my lawyer had for me was that just because the prosecutor recommends something doesn't necessarily mean the judge has to accept it. Either way, I felt better going to sentencing with these terms than if I had agreed on the original eleven-year recommendation. As hard as all this had been psychologically, I continued to work out, read the Bible, pray, and write my thoughts down for inner peace. Since being arrested and now clean, I had never been more grateful to be alive. It felt like I had awakened from a horrible nightmare. I truly believe even to this day as I write this that I was blessed with a second chance in life.

I received a piece of mail about a week or two later with my court date set for the beginning of February. This was it; everything I had been waiting for was finally here. Not to mention the fact that I had over one hundred days of being clean. It's mind-boggling to think about when you consider that I had been using drugs and alcohol since I was fifteen. Even at one hundred days clean I could notice a difference in my thinking. Big Country, on the other hand, had a whole other set of issues. Turns out he had legal mail as well. He had warrants in Minnesota for a felony DUI he had never cleared up. He was getting extradited.

My court date finally arrived. My mom, aunt, and two uncles were in court supporting me, even though I felt that my mom needed the support more than me. My mother faithfully visited and wrote letters to me every chance she could. One of the hardest things about being in jail was knowing what I put her and my family through. I could hear her crying from behind me in the courtroom, and it took everything in my power to hold back my tears. As much pain as I put myself through, I know it was harder on her and my family. During sentencing, the judge and prosecutor had some very stern words for me.

The prosecutor told the judge that I was a threat to myself and the community. She went on to tell the judge that I was a contributing factor to the influx of heroin and the heroin epidemic in the area. The judge looked at me before sentencing and said, "Why shouldn't I give you the maximum sentencing suggested?" He was referring to the eleven years that was first proposed by the prosecutor. He then went on to tell me how as a judge he had seen time after time how lives had been destroyed in his community from the heroin that had been coming in.

I replied by telling the judge I was relieved when I got arrested. I explained to him how I had struggled with heroin all through my twenties and that I just couldn't stop. I didn't know how to accept help. I told him that I understood the severity of my crimes and I was going to change my life. I told the judge that I truly believed getting arrested saved my life. Then I said, "You'll see, I'm going to change my life." He replied very sternly, "Don't do it for me, son, do it for yourself and do it for your family."

I believe God gave me the judge I had been praying for. I know I manifested this judge through my faith, knowing God has given us this ability to receive what we pray for. I prayed every night and every morning for a just, fair, and understanding judge, and that's exactly what I got that day. The judge took the prosecutor's recommendation, and I couldn't have been more relieved. I was just ready to start my prison sentence. After sentencing, my lawyer looked at me, shook my hand, and said, "I'll see you in a few years." I was able to talk to my family briefly in the hallway, but I was not allowed to hug my mom. The officer was very uptight and came across as behaving in a hasty manner.

In the county jail you're locked down twenty-three hours a day, seven days a week. My five months felt like a year. I think about how much had changed in those five months from detox to that moment, having over one hundred days clean. I was a completely different person just after this short amount of time. I'd watched seasons change through a window, and at times I felt there was no end in sight. Big Country's extradition took place, and it was bittersweet to see him go because I believed this was the last time I would see or hear from him for a few years at the least.

I felt sad because he had been my buddy since we were twelve. Even though we were grown now, there was still a piece of childhood memory tied to us. He was like a brother to me, and this was the direction our lives had taken? It's sad because neither of us had these plans for our lives when we were younger. Thinking back to riding our bikes on the trails and doing our paper routes, we were free-spirited and full of ambition back then. There had to be something better for us than a life of addiction and incarceration.

Addiction is the devil. It's some bullshit to think that we grow up and live in misery only to die filled with shame. We all need to wake up and embrace the desire to change. We need never lose sight of the good we can do in the world.

The dorm felt empty when Big Country left. As happy as I was that he was getting out of the county, I knew his next journey was just about to begin as well. I was sad that he was gone.

I didn't know what to expect from prison. In my mind, I was preparing to have to fight as soon as I got there. I had heard horror stories from guys in the county jail who had been to prison. None of the stories were good. All the guys I spoke to told me to pack light and be prepared to fight.

My time had come. I was called to pack everything up around six a.m. Before I left the dorm the corrections officer pulled me up to the desk and told me that he was proud of me and that I was going to be okay as long as I didn't lose the drive that I had now. He said out of every person in the dorm, he saw the most change out of me. He didn't know what it was about me, but he told me not to lose it. I looked him in the eyes, and with a smile I told him it was God.

Out in the main lobby in front of the intake I was shackled to another inmate and placed in a van. In total there were about seven of us. We were transported out about two hours north to Lorain, Ohio, for processing. In Ohio there are three prison reception centers. One is for women and the other two are for men. The location you are sent to for processing is dependent on the county of commitment. Because I was sentenced in northwest Ohio, I was shipped north. When I got to Lorain, the van pulled up to a compound that was surrounded by barbed wire and several sections of fencing.

We sat in the van for a good twenty minutes before the gate opened and we were allowed to drive through. We were escorted out of the van and taken into what looked like a garage-type

The Awakening

hangar. In there we were issued a uniform jumpsuit according to our sizes. I was stripped naked in a room with a group of twenty to thirty men. We were told to turn around, squat, and cough. I was all too familiar with this process as it was the institution's way of checking to see if anyone was attempting to bring in anything illegal. After this degrading process was over, we were ordered to put on our clothes. We waited in the cold room before being issued a net bag with sheets for the bed, travel-sized toothpaste and toothbrush, a bar of soap, and a roll of toilet paper. I thought to myself, *This is what my life has been reduced to?* I mean, it could have been worse; I could still be strung out.

Physically, I was feeling great compared to when I first detoxed from heroin. Mentally, though, even though I was feeling better, I could still notice the effects from years of drug use wearing off. I was still having a hard time with reading and retaining information. For instance, I still found myself losing attention as my mind would wander while reading. Regardless, I was eager to get this process over with, as I just wanted to get to my cell. It was mentally draining, and I wanted to get to a phone to at least call home and let my mom know I had made it to processing. Even though it was a processing center, it was still in fact a prison. The inmates who were doing their prison sentence here were housed in different buildings from the processing part of the facility.

Next, we were shuffled through a hallway to a barbershop, where our heads were shaved, and then moved down the hallway for pictures. This is when you are entered into the system and given your prison number ID badge. To put things in perspective, my number started with a six, and it was six digits long. Years later, before my release, there were guys with numbers starting in the eights. That's a lot of people passing through the prison system.

4.
The Transformation

Once in my cell, I didn't even get unpacked before I realized the room was freezing. It was snowing outside, and the air was blowing through the cracks of the window frame. I could see my breath in the air. The cell was filthy, and curse words were written all over the walls, doors, and ceiling. The word *FUCK* was written across the ceiling in huge letters. Gangs and people's names, along with other random ramblings, had been written on the walls too. Memories of borderline mental breakdowns were scribbled on the door along with makeshift calendars marked out in pencil. I could feel the sorrow inside these four walls.

This cell was dirty and depressing, and there was a brown substance that looked like feces smeared on the vents. There also looked to be toilet paper that had been soaked with water at one point or another and thrown against the wall, but was now dried and caked to the vent. It was absolutely foul. I believe this place was designed to break you down and defeat you if you let it. It was a test, and I knew it was, but I persevered. I prayed over the room, and I spoke light into this darkness. I refused to succumb to the pain that had been left behind in this cell.

God got me through my detox and built me up stronger than I had ever been. I wasn't going to lose sight of that. I had come too far, and I knew that this was just the beginning.

During my first week in Lorain, I received mail from a close friend of mine, Jordan. If I were to sum up how far back he and I go, I would say fishing poles and bicycles. I have many fond memories of growing up and fishing with him. "Raising some cane," as the old saying goes.

Seriously, though, what kid in the early '90s didn't spend most of their time outside running around and riding bikes? During my time in Pittsburgh, Jordan was in prison, and I wrote to him a few times, but now the role was reversed, and here he was writing to me because I was the one who was incarcerated. It's crazy how tables can turn in the blink of an eye. This letter wasn't one I was expecting. It was needed, though. By the time I moved home from Pittsburgh, Jordan had already been out of prison for several years and had graduated from college with a bachelor's in civil engineering.

He was doing very well for himself in Columbus, Ohio. I was already back into using heroin heavily when Jordan called me on the phone one day out of the blue. We were talking, and he had mentioned a sober living house he stayed at when he first got out of prison. The house was called Serenity Street, but I wasn't ready for that commitment, and so I didn't take him up on the offer.

Now fast-forward several years, and he was writing to me as I sat in prison. His letter was uplifting and encouraging. He wrote to tell me he had sent money to help with hygiene and for whatever else I needed in order to get me through. He knew I was only going to be there for a short time and told me what to expect in Lorain. He also advised me to have my family look into filing for hardship for a closer institution. He also referenced Marion Correctional because it was the closest to my mom.

You just never know where you're going to end up in life, and success isn't always defined by perfection. Perseverance plays just as much of a role in all of it. During the second week in processing, I found out my family had finally written to the director of prisons and properly requested a hardship. They did exactly what Jordan said they should do. My family filed asking to have me placed at Marion Correctional. By the grace of God, the request was granted. It took a few weeks, but when I found out where I was going, it was like hitting the lottery. The prison was only forty-five minutes away from my mom, which beat the two-hour drive she was making now. I was officially going to Marion Correctional. An interesting fact about this institution at the time was that out of all the prisons in Ohio, Marion had the most programs geared toward preparing men for a successful reentry.

During my stay at Lorain, the thing that stood out to me the most during processing was my experience with the caseworker. The lady asked me if I wanted to be an organ donor. I was thrown off by that question and asked why that mattered. The caseworker stopped typing, looked me dead in my eyes, and said, "In case you die while you're in prison." It just never occurred to me that I might possibly die while in prison. I understood how that could be an outcome—you know, gang violence or whatever—but it never really dawned on me even while I was in county jail. Talk about naivete. My time in Lorain lasted about a month before I finally made it to Marion Correctional. In March 2012, I was on the bus by five a.m. and didn't get off until later that morning.

As the bus pulled up to the prison, it was the same layout as Lorain, with the fencing and barbed wire. I didn't know what to expect from prison. A part of me knew I was going to have to protect myself if needed, but at the same time, I wasn't some badass off the streets. I couldn't even tell you the last time I had been in a fist fight with someone. I never really was a confrontational person growing up, so naturally, this aspect of prison made me nervous. I was hopeful about being at Marion because of the programs it had to offer. I was unsure about the living conditions and was hoping that it wasn't going to be anything like Lorain.

Nonetheless, there was a level of caution as I got off the bus that I wasn't willing to shake at the time. I kept thinking about the saying "pack light in case you fight"; after all, I was in prison. After everyone was off the bus, the sergeant and correctional officers unshackled us. I recall hearing the sergeant telling everyone not to take kindness as a weakness. Given the situation I was in at the time, I thought that comment was weird, but I wasn't trying to think too much about it. I just wanted to find out where I was going and get to my bed and unpack.

We were led to the laundry department, where I was issued my uniforms. Then the corrections officers started calling out our names individually. Once everyone was accounted for, we were split into several different groups and told to follow the guards. We were led down a long brick hallway where hundreds of other men were walking to get to the cafeteria. Men were standing in line in the hallway waiting for the commissary, and they even headed out to the recreational yard. It was an overwhelmingly chaotic first impression. The brick hallways were the glazed tile bricks from the '50s, and you could feel the history just by looking at the floor and walls. This institution was bigger on the inside than it appeared to be from the outside.

I couldn't help but think about how many people had passed through this place. After what felt like a mile of walking down this extremely long hallway, I finally got to my dorm. The housing units were called dorms. All the units were equivalent to a half basketball court with four rows of bunk beds. Each dorm housed close to 250 men, and the compound population was around three thousand at the time.

It was a strange feeling walking into the dorm, not knowing a single person. You heard music playing, and you smelled cigarettes, and it felt like everyone was staring at you. Being one of the new guys coming into the dorm, there was a sense of silence I picked up on, even though it was loud. The best way I can explain it is that you could feel tension in the air. I know they were trying to get a read on me, and all I kept thinking to myself was to stand tall but don't come off as being cocky. Just get to your bed area and get situated, and everything else would work itself out.

I knew I looked like a deer in the headlights. I needed to use the phone and call home, but first, I just needed to get situated and then figure everything else out. I got to my bunk, and of course, as luck would have it, I was on the top rack. I was kind of hoping I would have a bottom bunk, but beggars can't be choosers. As I unpacked and made my bed, I began to go through all my paperwork just to make sure I still had everything from the transfer. I started talking to my bunkie, the guy on the bottom bunk. I asked about lunch, because I was hungry.

Turned out I had missed lunch. Dinner wasn't for another couple of hours. He asked me what I was in prison for, and I told him it was for drug trafficking. I asked him the same question back. He replied by saying, "Same, drug trafficking." My bunkie had a bunch of books, like he was studying for something, so I asked him if it was hard to get into programs. He told me there were plenty of programs and that they weren't too hard to get into. He said I just needed to find which ones I wanted to be in, then have my case manager put my name on a waiting list.

I was already starting to work on figuring out what I could do to get my time moving. There were so many things going through my head at the same time. Once dinner was finished, I got back to the dorm and was able to make a phone call and talk to my mom. I let her know I had made it to Marion and that everything was okay. She told me she would schedule a visitation to come see me as soon as she could. A few days later, during count time, the corrections officer came to me with a hall pass, telling me to report to the chapel after count.

Count time is when everyone returns to their dorms or cells and must sit on their beds for a head count. This is done to determine that everyone is accounted for in the compound.

For security purposes, I'm not going to give a detailed list of when the counts are done. I will tell you there is a count time at breakfast, lunch, and dinner. During count time, the guys told me that it usually isn't good to be called to the chapel if you're not expecting it. It usually means there was a death in the family.

After count time I headed down to the chapel with a bit of concern. I was thinking that it wasn't going to be good. I got to the chaplain's office, and he told me to come in. As I entered his office, I noticed off to the side in the corner of the room sat my friend Jordan. I couldn't believe it. I was blown away that Jordan had a visitor's pass to come in and see me. Turns out he was there for one of the ministry programs he had graduated from, and he was able to get me a pass to come down to the chapel. Words couldn't explain how I felt to see him that day after so many years. I thanked the chaplain for the pass, and he encouraged me to swing by during the week to see if there were any programs I might be interested in taking.

I just couldn't stop smiling—it was amazing to be able to see a familiar face. While Jordan and I visited, he reassured me that he was there to support me through this chapter in my life. I thanked him for the money and for writing to me. He told me to keep an eye out for a ministry program that was going to start. He told me that I needed to sign up for it. The program was called Embark, which was a nonprofit prison ministry program designed to work with men and women one year before they were expected to be released. The program provided housing for up to one year after they were released from prison.

Embark members met with the men and women on specific days throughout each month, going over workbooks that were provided. Each individual participant was given assignments during each class. The men and women went over everything in the groups the next time that class met. The programs that Embark provided were *Getting It Right* and *Celebrate Recovery*. *Getting It Right* was a cognitive behavioral therapy workbook geared toward providing fundamental learning theory. It was based on hypothetical scenarios individuals might face once released.

For example, they helped with peer pressure, problem-solving high-stress situations, and even financial planning. These were done individually as homework but discussed as a group. *Celebrate Recovery* was a twelve-step program based on scriptures and principles from the Bible. We discussed the material and worked together as a group. To me, this literature was a form of journaling. The only difference was that you shared your answers with your group.

After hearing these details about the program, I was excited to see when the registration was going to take place. It was another opportunity I knew would prepare me for reentry. After all, that's what everyone in prison wanted. We all wanted to come home. I remember when Jordan called me years before my arrest and suggested the opportunity for me to go into sober living. Had I taken that offer at the time, I could only imagine where I would be in life now. Instead, I ignored that opportunity, and there I was in prison. I wasn't going to pass on his suggestion this time around.

I had never been more open-minded for guidance and suggestions than now. I loved the challenge life was giving me, because it allowed me to grow. It gave me hope and allowed me to see beyond my incarceration. It fueled my drive for a better life.

My first week at Marion came to an end, and in conclusion, I was able to sign up for a long list of programs geared toward stress management, recovery, and faith. Each day after signing up for classes or going to recovery meetings, I spent the rest of my time working out when possible. After six months of confinement in county jail and in Lorain, being outside gave me a sense of freedom.

The Transformation

The prison yard was my way to get away from being inside. The yard was open every day for several hours at a time after each count time and meals. The only time the yard would be closed was if there was fog or if the prison was on lockdown. If the prison was on lockdown, it was usually for search-and-seizures or gang issues. Those situations didn't happen a lot at Marion. If they did happen, it was only a couple of times a year. Mostly it was weather-related. Since my arrest, I was determined to take every opportunity I could to embrace change. My first weekend in prison wasn't bad, and oddly enough, the whole institution seemed to have a sense of rhythm about it. I noticed weekends were quieter than during the week, and once I started to get used to how people were moving around, it became my rhythm as well.

I went out on the yard that Saturday morning, and out of several thousand inmates on the compound, there were probably only fifty guys walking the track. Everyone else was still sleeping in. That morning, it was nice to see the sun and watch it dry the dew off the fields on the other side of the fence. The yard had a quarter-mile track with two baseball diamonds and several basketball courts. At first, I started walking around the track one full lap, then I started to jog. My jog turned into a run, and before I knew it, I had this urge to keep running. I felt like I had all this energy consuming me after being locked up in county jail and Lorain for so long.

I felt good about my first week in Marion, and I was motivated for the weekend to end so that I could get back into my new weekly routine. The weekends were slow. Most if not all of the programming didn't take place over the weekends, as staff were not in on the weekends to run the programs. The only ones there were the guards. I went to church that Sunday and sat in the back, where I listened to the sermon. I was surprised by the sermon and the choir. I was impressed by the guys who were singing. They had a passion for it, and I could sense that something was spiritually different about this place. I went back to the dorm motivated and inspired for my week to start.

I remember walking back to the dorm, reminding myself of how good the message was. The following week came around, and one morning, when I woke up at five a.m. to get ready for breakfast, my neighbor told me that a guy was standing at the foot of my bed, smelling my feet. I was thinking that he was joking with me, but then the tone in his voice changed. He told me, "Dude, I'm not playing you. You're going to have to handle this because that dude was smelling your feet. He's a repeat sex offender!" I knew who the guy was—everyone in the dorm did. He was a very socially awkward individual who was well known for being a sexual predator. It was just best not to even engage with guys like that.

Up to this point, I had no interactions with him. You become aware of who is who within your surroundings and do your best to stay safe. You have to; it's part of surviving prison. You learn how people carry themselves and how they move. You learn their demeanor. You learn who to look out for and who to stay away from. It's imperative to know who not to get involved with. I was pissed, and at the same time I was wondering, *Am I being set up to fight or something?* I went to breakfast, and on my way back to the dorm, I was thinking that I was going to have to fight this guy if he tried to confront me. I didn't want to fight; I just wanted to do my time and come home. I also wasn't going to let anyone harm me. When I got back to the dorm, that dude was standing by my bed area.

I thought to myself, *Are you fucking kidding me?* That's when I knew shit had just gotten real. The first words out of this guy's mouth were, "Hey, young blood. I know you just got here, but are you trying to work out today?"

I said, "No, I'm good."

Like I said, the guy was socially awkward, and he just stood there and stared at me through his Coke bottle glasses for a few seconds. He stared at me with his beady little eyes and then asked me what my problem was.

I replied, "Look, man, I don't have a problem. I don't know you, and I really don't care to know you. Do me a favor and stay away from my area."

The guy started to get loud with me as he turned around to walk away and said, "Meet me in the bathroom, BITCH!"

I replied, "I'm not going anywhere. Stay in your *fucking lane* and BACK OFF!"

He kept walking back to his bed area, and it looked like he grabbed something from under his mattress. As he proceeded to walk back toward me, he had this aggression in his steps as he yelled from across the dorm room, "Fuck you and your white bolt friends!" All the while he kept his hand in his shirt.

I looked at my neighbor, who was standing there watching everything unfold, and I thought to myself, *I'm about to get in a fight.* This whole situation was crazy, unexpected, and awkward. As I write about this part of my journey, I've contemplated whether to even include it. I've struggled with people-pleasing and wondering what the reader might think. I've thought to myself, *What are my peers going to think when they read this?*

Some may read this and have a different vision of how they may have handled it. Some may judge me and think I acted cowardly for not smashing the dude's skull in. Trust me, I've replayed a million different scenarios of how this situation could have been different. In the end, I just wanted to go home. Was I scared? Hell, yes. But I stood my ground for what I felt was an appropriate demand for respect.

He started getting loud again and made a huge scene as he stopped and kept his hand inside his shirt. I thought he was about to try and stab me or something, but he never got any closer. Instead, he stood about four feet from me. The next thing I knew, I heard the corrections officer yell my name and tell me, "Get in the hall!" All this happened right as I was expecting him to try and swing on me, but he didn't. The guy turned around and walked away, and I walked out into the hallway. The guard told me to go to the sergeant's office.

This whole time, all I could think of was not getting into trouble. I just wanted to do my time and file for my judicial release in four years. At the same time, I wasn't about to stand for any kind of violence. I was going to do everything I could to protect myself.

When I got to the unit sergeant's office, she asked me what was going on. I told her, "Nothing. It was just a misunderstanding." She clicked her pen a few times on her desk while looking at her computer. She said, "You've been here two weeks and are already getting into misunderstandings. I'm not gonna deal with it on my wing. I'm moving you to another dorm." Then she said, "Don't let me see you in my office again."

I went back to the dorm, packed all my belongings, and moved to the new dorm. I didn't know what to think at the time. It was the craziest sequence of events, but then again, I was also in prison so…

The new dorm turned out to be wild. I was placed in dorm five. In the prison, it was referred to as the "dirty nickel." These guys were making hooch and hiding it in the walls in the shower area. Guys smoked weed and cigarettes, and my neighbor was getting tattoos.

Over the next few weeks, I was still kind of pissed about my encounter with the creepy foot smeller. There were a few guys I met when I first got to prison who were familiar with my situation in the first dorm. Despite the inside joke of calling me "twinkle toes," they were also trying to convince me that I needed to finish what was started. I remember one conversation where I was told prison wasn't the same as on the streets. These problems don't resolve themselves; you have to finish what was started. If you don't handle the problem, the problem will handle you. It was at this point that I had it in my head that I was going to put a hit out on the guy. Food was the bartering system, and it was as good as cash. For the right price, the message was going to be clear.

One weekend in the dirty nickel, these guys were drinking and fighting all through the night. I came back from the cafeteria after dinner on a Friday evening, and they had the music blasting. They were smoking cigarettes and getting tattoos in the back of the dorm. I thought to myself, *This place is nuts*. If I remember correctly, the corrections officers were called to our dorm three times that night for fights. I didn't care, though, because it wasn't any of my business.

I was just glad to have good neighbors. We looked out for each other's area, which was a form of respect. In prison, you have all walks of life sleeping in the same dorm as you. Murderers, rapists, sex offenders—old and young. Thieves, drug addicts, drug dealers, violent offenders, and gang members. To have good neighbors is a blessing, to say the least. A lot of time is spent in the dorms, so the one thing you want is to establish respect among your neighbors. If not, you're going to have a hard time.

I just continued to go to recovery meetings during the week and also got into a few morning Bible programs. The Bible studies helped me focus more deeply on my relationship with God. I met a few men who were doing life while going to the Bible groups. They shared their pasts and how they came from dark places in life. They spoke about when they converted their lives to Christ and why. You wouldn't even know that these guys were doing life sentences if you had met them in society. I mean, they had made a complete transformation, based on the stories they shared about their pasts.

That was great motivation for me, and it was where I saw the potential for God in my life. It was there in prison that I heard for the first time in thirty years of my life, "God has a plan for you. He is going to use you in a mighty way." It was something that hit my soul, as if I had been yearning to hear that my whole life. Maybe I had. Maybe in some kind of crazy, twisted way, a part of me was there because I needed to hear that. All I know is that I took that statement and held onto it and never lost sight of it. To this day, I'm reminded of the brother who professed that into my life, and I will never forget it.

Time went by quickly in prison because I was staying busy. Before I knew it, two months had gone by since I'd switched dorms. Occasionally, I still saw my old neighbors in the hallways or in the yard. One day, while out in the yard, I saw a guy from the first dorm I was in. He proceeded to tell me that the guy who had smelled my feet tried to pull a young boy into the mop closet and rape him. A bunch of guys from Cleveland jumped in and beat that dude to the point where he was sent to the medical infirmary. The boy's parents called the prison and raised a lot of concerns to the investigator and the warden. They were concerned about what had happened to their son and how something like that could happen in an open dorm.

Apparently, after everything took place, the rapist was sent to a maximum-security facility, where he should have been all along. I felt bad for that kid. It turned out the kid was borderline special needs. It just really solidified the type of person the creepy foot smeller really was. You hear of prison stories that turn out way worse for individuals, and I'm just glad nothing bad happened to that kid. I was even more grateful I didn't get stabbed. The biggest lesson I learned from that situation was to always be aware of my surroundings. I mean, why else would that guy have gone back to his bed and returned with his hand in his shirt if he didn't have a knife?

I think the guards were already aware of this individual's character and his potential, which is why they didn't have him in a cell. After that, a rumor was going around that the guy had caught a rape charge at the new institution he was sent to. All I could do was thank God for looking out for me. I could have been stabbed in my sleep or right where I stood, arguing with him that day. In the end, I know God intervened, and I never had to follow through with paying to have the guy beat up.

In September 2012, I officially celebrated my first year clean. I was able to share at a meeting about what I'd learned from the Narcotics Anonymous literature. My sponsor chaired the weekly meetings and had been working with me a lot to get me to my fifth step.

During the meeting, I shared with everyone the thing that had stood out the most in my first year of being clean. The literature tells us that each and every one of us who has been able to stop using and pick up the "Twelve Steps" book is a "miracle." If that isn't inspiring, then I don't know what else is. I AM A MIRACLE. Say that to yourself until you believe it, because it's still true. When I started using drugs, I was fifteen. When I got arrested, I was thirty, and now I was thirty-one with one year clean.

The math is simple. I had been using drugs for half of my life. For the first time in my adult life, I was thinking clearly. It's humbling to be able to say that. What's even greater is when you're able to identify what you're feeling instead of allowing your anger to determine your next decisions. The next month, in October, things were starting to slow down. It seemed that because the weather was changing, I wasn't able to get outside as much because of the rain. The reality of a five-year prison term was starting to kick in.

Everything was going well for me with the classes I was taking. I was just starting to feel the effects of prison in a deeper way than when I first got there. One October morning, I went outside just to reflect and clear my head, and it was cold, dark, and cloudy outside. Not many people were out on the yard that day. I sat on a bench by myself, and I was feeling depressed. Then I started praying and thanking God.

I started talking to God and telling him how I was feeling, and I asked for guidance and strength to get me through these next few years. I got really overwhelmed and started to tell God I was sorry. I started crying and repeatedly saying I was sorry for all the pain I had caused and for all the people I had hurt. At that point, I just asked God to give me a sign because I didn't feel like I was being heard. I felt alone and ashamed and extremely isolated. Next thing I knew, as I was walking through the field, the sun came out from the dark clouds over me.

The clouds rolled back, and blue skies began to appear. The clouds were so thick and had such a defined edge that it literally looked like a carpet being rolled up. The experience was so profound to me, because while I was praying, this supernatural event was happening right before my eyes. I believe God revealed his presence in my life again at that moment. I immediately began looking around to see if I was the only one experiencing this phenomenon. I instantly felt emotionally relieved. It reminded me of when I prayed in my bedroom a year back, asking God for help. I knew I needed to stay focused on my recovery and my relationship with God. I knew this was unequivocally God answering me.

This whole experience took place within an hour, and as I went back in for count time, I had a renewed sense of my circumstances. Everything was even clearer now. Just keep working the twelve steps, keep taking personal development classes, and keep digging deeper into my relationship with God. At this point, I'd been at Marion for seven months. For the last six months, I had been trying to get into the Recovery Services dorm. What was so unique about this dorm was that it had programs offered directly in the dorm with a population half the size of the dorm I was in at the time.

I would be around people who were going to recovery meetings, unlike the guys I was used to being around. What I mean is, the guys in the dirty nickel were not going to recovery meetings or going to church. They were shooting tattoos, making hooch, and smoking weed. The recovery dorm in my mind was the best of all prison dorms, if there ever was one. I applied several different times over seven months. I had even spoken to the Recovery Services staff about getting into the recovery dorm on multiple occasions.

Every time I inquired about the dorm, I was met with rejection. To be considered, you had to have less than five years left on your sentence. I believed I would be a great candidate and role model for that dorm, since I was active in all the recovery programs offered at Marion. I felt I would be a great fit, not to mention my mandatory time was under five years. As I continued my regular attendance in the Recovery Services department, I also started attending programs offered in the mental health department. The first program I learned about through mental health was from another inmate. The class was called Dual Diagnosis, and it was through this class that I met a psychologist and therapist by the name of Mr. C.

This instructor was different. He would engage in meaningful conversations and talk to us about psychology, meditation, and music. He was a very laid-back guy. It was through him that I first got exposed to meditating and guided meditation. It was an unorthodox approach that I wasn't used to, but I was interested. I believe that my openness to expand my mind was what allowed me to benefit the most from his approach to therapy.

I learned how to identify whether or not throughout the day I was subconsciously clenching my jaw, which was an indicator of stress. I learned that if I were able to stay mindful in my thoughts, I would be able to reduce the stress. I learned that by taking ten deep breaths and clearing my mind, I was able to release the stress. While taking Mr. C's stress management course and completing Dual Diagnosis, Mr. C told me he was looking into creating more programs and asked if I would be interested in being his clerk. I accepted the opportunity and was extremely excited that he considered me for this.

It was about mid-October when I was told to pack up my stuff because I was moving. I was thrown off by the news and surprised by it. I wasn't expecting to hear that and kind of didn't believe it at first. I asked the CO where I was going, and he told me the recovery dorm. I was so happy it was hard to keep a straight face.

My old belief systems were in line with things never working out in my favor. Since I've been clean, though, it's proven to be the exact opposite. Positive things continued to happen for me. When I got to the dorm, it had a fish tank in it. Another nice thing about the new dorm was that we were allowed to make thirty-minute phone calls rather than fifteen-minute calls, and they had a Nintendo Wii. Those things were nice and all, but the greatest thing was the single beds, which meant no more bunkie. I was just happy because it felt like I was able to breathe a little more.

I met the unit manager, Mrs. S. One thing I valued about how she handled things was her open-door policy. I was able to talk to her about my recovery, and she was engaging in conversations. I didn't know it at the time, but Mrs. S would turn out to play a key role in the rest of my time at Marion Correctional. I believe God places people in our lives when you least expect it. There was a level of professionalism that she possessed that I thought was balanced between a policy of caring and no bullshit, which I respected.

It was Thanksgiving time, and before I knew it, Christmas rolled around again. It seemed like every time I called home, my mom was telling me someone else had passed away from a heroin overdose. Within two months, five people died whom I used to get high with. It was the first time since coming to prison that people I used to know were dying from heroin.

I was already convinced that incarceration had saved my life, but the loss of so many people in such a short amount of time just solidified the fact of how close I was to dying. I remember taking an inventory of how it affected me emotionally. I made an observation and wrote it down in a journal I was keeping. In my writings, I would describe the situations that were affecting me positively and negatively. I would write about how I would have handled things in the past, and I would compare those choices to how I was addressing my thoughts and feelings while in prison.

Had I still been using drugs back then, I would have just gotten high again. Now I was praying and working out and going to meetings. Around the same time I got to the recovery dorm, my Narcotics Anonymous sponsor got his judicial release and was headed back to Cleveland. Selfishly I didn't want to see him go, because this was my first time working the steps. In my opinion, he was the best sponsor on the compound.

I ended up mailing my fifth step to him, and at first, I didn't think he would write back, but I mailed it anyway. The fifth step is: We admitted to God, ourselves, and another human being the exact nature of our wrongs. This was a big step for me, and it took me some time to get through it. I was looking forward to clearing my plate from my toxic past.

I went all the way back to my childhood. I had a very troubled past. There was a lot of yelling and a lot of emotional pain growing up. I didn't hold any punches, though; I wrote it all out. I felt like if I was going to do this right, I was going to have to uncover all of it. It was a very personal step, and I felt like I was being robbed of it because I couldn't share it with him in person.

I realized that as much as the fifth step was about me, it really wasn't. I needed to appreciate the fact that my sponsor was going home to start his new life. That in and of itself was great to experience. In the meantime, I continued to study the twelve-step literature.

I kept going to meetings several times a week so I could get to know the guys in the dorm better. One of the guys who stood out to me and became a close friend of mine was Mark. I always joked that he was the prison version of Adam Levine, the lead singer from the band Maroon 5. He was very intelligent and talented. He could play guitar, sing, and had a heck of a sense of humor.

Regardless of all these qualities, though, Mark had a lot of work he needed to do on his recovery. I only say this because at the time, he wasn't open to the fact that he needed to work the steps in order to get better. Mark was a dirt-bike-riding country boy and an air force veteran. He struggled with crack and ended up in prison. His addictions led him to rob cab drivers, store clerks, and people at ATMs in front of grocery stores. Despite admitting all his failures, he felt that he could fix his issues on his own and didn't need AA or NA. We spent a lot of time together and had many conversations about why it was important to do the twelve steps. He reminded me of myself before I got arrested. I knew I had a problem, but I wasn't willing to admit that I needed to do the work to get to the core of it all.

All I could do was lead by example so that others could see how I was working the steps. In the end, he eventually came around to working the steps with a sponsor. I was happy for him and told him I was proud of him. I never implied that he had to work the steps with me. Instead, I told him I would be there as a friend to support him if he ever had any questions.

My time in the recovery dorm didn't last as long as I had anticipated, though. March 2013 rolled around exactly a year from the time I first got to Marion. My security level was lowered, and I was sent out to the camp. The camp was still on the compound, but it was in a separate facility. It was referred to as "the camp" because the guys out there were able to go outside the fence to work. I was completely thrown off by this move and didn't think that I would make it outside the fence for anything other than my trip back home to see the judge for release. Nevertheless, here I was moving once again.

One Year Clean

This time last year, I was clean 24 hours,
feeling like hell refusing food and showers.
In the moment I was powerless to the pain,
the experience was terrible, and I was filled with shame.
There were no fingers to point, no one to blame,
the time had come for me to make a change.
At my rock bottom I asked God for help.
He picked me up and said, "Decide for yourself."
Thank You, God, for a second chance at life.
Today, I'm stronger, and You showed me your light.
You waited for me to ask for help.
You knew I would choose you, refusing this hell.
I know I was wrong, and I'm sorry for that.
Help me stay strong so I'll never go back.
The heroin had me sick, I was on the dark side of the moon,
Desolate and cold, secluded in my room.
Just for today, I'm clean, I'm alive.
Thank You, God, for a new way of life.

5.

One Step Closer

My transition to the camp was a turning point for me during my incarceration. I looked at it as a stepping stone toward being able to come home from prison in a couple of years. It represented a growing pain, because on one hand, I was having to switch up the way I was doing my time. On the other hand, it was also a new chapter in my life. It allowed me to create a routine for more classes, and I was embracing this new change. Once again, I had to reestablish myself in a dorm filled with people I didn't know. Moving in, I was just unsure of what to expect. Just because I was at a lowered level of security at the camp, it didn't mean I wasn't going to have to deal with new challenges. Nonetheless, I came in open-minded and hopeful that this new move would be positive.

Prison is filled with uncertainties, which is why having a routine helps with doing time. Being out at the new facility brought me a sense of freedom in an environment where I had none. Being given a gate pass to go outside the fence didn't happen right away. Instead, I was given the job of cleaning the bathrooms every day during afternoon count time. The camp was divided into two sections. The only difference between the two sides was that one side of the building was geared for reintegration, allowing guys more reentry classes.

Once I got situated at the camp, I realized nothing really changed as far as how the facility was run. We still had the same count times and the same food. We did have a pool table, though, and we were allowed to go downstairs after the evening count for a few more hours.

The environment was definitely different. From what I understood about being out at the camp, I was going to be able to start classes that I had been waiting to get into. Classes such as Thinking for a Change, Anger Management, and a few others that were geared around cognitive behavioral therapy (CBT). For me, the two most important programs that I had been waiting for were Intensive Outpatient (IOP) and Alcohol and Other Drugs (AOD), which were both recovery-services related.

For me, these were the big ones because they were both federally and state-recognized. For each program that I took, I received a certificate, and I kept those certificates. I saved these certificates so that when I filed for my judicial release, I could send them to my lawyer for the judge. I wanted to show that my time in prison wasn't wasted. In July I found out through the Recovery Services department that Mr. C had passed away from cancer. The news was so abrupt and unexpected that when it finally kicked in, it made me sad. I never knew he was sick, let alone that he was dying.

Mr. C showed no emotion to reveal the fact that he knew his fate. Instead, he showed up to work and provided his knowledge selflessly. The fact that he saw something in me, even with all his health issues, helped me understand a deeper purpose in life. It was an honor to have met him and to receive the last bit of knowledge he had to share before his passing. When I moved out to the camp in the spring, he came out and visited me to see how my transition was. He explained to me that he was still working on getting me hired as his assistant, and he gave me a copy of the book *The 7 Habits of Highly Effective People*.

This book was just the first of many other books that helped me tap into a deeper understanding of my true potential. That was the last time I saw Mr. C. Prison is an emotional battle. You try your hardest to stay in the realm of logic and work on doing the time and not letting the time do you. My perception of myself and time shifted. I no longer looked at myself as I once had when I was strung out on drugs. I've learned to believe in myself in a way I never thought was possible. Time feels like more of a concept than a reality now. I no longer worry about the time like I once did. Unless I am dealing with an appointment, time is now more a counting of seasons. I used to count the hours and quickly found out that this approach could lead to insanity. A separation of your emotions happens by force when the acceptance of long-term incarceration sets in. However, in this instance with Mr. C, my time briefly stopped, and I allowed his passing to affect how I was feeling. I will never forget this man.

After I mailed my fifth step to my previous sponsor, he wrote me back. He encouraged me to find someone in prison to sponsor me. I knew this was the probable outcome and had already been working on finding someone new. I wrote him back thanking him, and I told him that I had made it out to the camp. The fact that my first sponsor reviewed my step work and wrote me back was a solid thing to do. He didn't have to write me, but he did. My new sponsor was Terry, and he worked as the Recovery Services clerk. He shared early on that he had been in and out of prison multiple times throughout his life.

My focus wasn't on how many times he had returned to prison. My focus was on what he was sharing in the meetings and the things that didn't work for him each time he went home. I was willing to listen, because the way he was able to break down the literature helped me to understand where I may end up if I began to get complacent with doing the step work. He was my sponsor the rest of my time in prison, and he even helped me when I started sponsoring guys.

It took me two years before I started sponsoring other guys. There was a time when I had hit a low point with the men I was helping. I went back to Terry and explained to him I needed to go back through the twelve steps. I believed I was doing something wrong as a sponsor. I explained to him that every guy I worked the steps with stopped on the third one. The third step is: "We make a decision to turn our will and our lives over to the care of God."

Terry explained to me that not everyone is comfortable with being powerless, not to mention giving it over to God. Especially if they feel that God has abandoned them.

That's why it's called working the steps. You have to work to get through the steps. He explained to me that it's normal, and "all you can do is be willing to share what you know and support them."

He also said, "The third step takes time, but the fourth step is even harder, so don't beat yourself up." This was valuable advice, and it helped me grow in my recovery. Eventually, I was moved over to the reintegration side of the camp and became more active in helping the guys who wanted to work their steps. The first year at the camp flew by, and before I knew it, I was looking at 2014 rapidly approaching. I was excited about it because my time at Marion was starting to add up, which meant my time in prison was getting shorter.

That December, I got a letter in the mail from Big Country. Apparently, he was in prison for ninety days. He had gotten into trouble for a CPO probation violation again, and instead of staying on probation he decided to finish up his time in prison. I couldn't fault him in his approach, but my thought was: *Dude, you had ninety days left.* Even though it was his decision, I personally couldn't understand his approach. I would rather have just stuck it out and not have to go through the prison system. It was nice hearing from him, though, and being able to write to him. I shared with him my clean time, and he explained to me his whole ordeal from when he was extradited.

Turned out they had taken him all the way to Minnesota just to drop the charges on some kind of technicality. *What a waste of time and resources,* I thought. He told me he was proud of me and was asking what I planned to do when I got home. I told him I was moving to Columbus for better opportunities. I had already begun to lay out several game plans to ensure a successful reentry. I explained to him that Jordan, whom we both knew, told me about his reentry plans when he got home from prison. He had a list from A to Z, and none of those plans had worked for him. He never gave up, though. He told me you have to keep on keepin' on.

I was also at a point in my recovery where I decided it was time to start working on making amends to people from my past. In doing so I was able to write to Amelia's mother, and I apologized for the pain that was caused by me and her two daughters during our drug use. My ex and I had a really bad falling out because of our addiction. Her family struggled with getting the girls into recovery after Amelia and I first separated. Come to find out through writing the girls' mother, eventually my ex ended up graduating college for something in the medical field.

Mia, on the other hand, continued to struggle with active addiction just like I did. When I wrote to her mother I expressed that my intentions for writing were out of my deepest respect for her. I explained to her that if anyone deserved an apology it was her. She was such a caring woman and saw nothing but the best in me even at my worst. The least I could do was write to her for the purpose of closure. I'm sure it sounds like I was thinking of myself, but in order for me to get better I needed to let go of the past. I told her I didn't expect her to write back and that I wished her the best in life because she deserved that.

I was definitely going through a transformational phase during this time. I was focusing on my reentry plans and digging deep into my recovery. My whole approach was to put as much of the past behind me before I came home. I wanted my main focus to be on the present instead of allowing the past to hold me back. With that in mind I was really thinking of a career in recovery. My plan was to get certified as a peer support in a Recovery Services facility.

Some of the guys told me I was being naive for thinking about preparing now because it wasn't going to make a difference.

I brushed it off. Those opinions are synonymous with people who have a *lack* mindset and low standards for themselves. As insensitive as it may sound, that kind of thinking is what creates a limited mindset. It made more sense for me to prepare for reentry now than to sit around and do nothing.

I thought I would be good at working with people who were still struggling with addiction. Who else better to work with people in recovery than someone who has been through it? As I continued to work on my writings, I slowly began to accumulate a decent amount of entries from my journaling. During the holidays that year I came up with the idea to write a book. I thought to myself, *It makes perfect sense to share my story and my thoughts.* My neighbor, whom I had become close to through Bible study, seemed to like the idea about a book as well.

My neighbor was just another confirmation of God putting people in my life early on. "Brother Maine," as I referred to him, was always reading and studying the Bible. I felt a calling to pay attention to him when he spoke, and I started asking him questions from time to time. Eventually he began to do studies with me. He started teaching the King James version of the Bible to me. At times he would use a concordance to help us in navigating specific words used in the King James version. I liked this because the concordance gives you a deeper understanding of thinking when reading scripture. The concordance allows the user to look up the meaning to the Greek word in the associated dictionary, showing how the original word was translated into the English form.

Since before coming to prison, I could testify that God had moved in mighty ways in my life. Since getting arrested and going to prison, though, there have been many other occurrences of Him revealing His awesomeness in my life, which I have shared. Another example of this was when Brother Maine and I were studying the Old Testament. Two hours flew by, and it felt like twenty minutes. We started at one p.m., and next thing we knew it was 3:30. We both had a look on our faces llike, *What the heck just happened?* I kid you not, the passing of time was so strange for both of us that there was no doubt that this was something more supernatural. To this day my experiences and growth with Brother Maine were just another example of God working in my life. It was like time froze but fast-forwarded at the same time.

    The changes I was experiencing were rewarding and humbling. I knew there were people out there still struggling and feeling the way I used to feel from heroin addiction. Not to mention other addictions. Today I understand that I have purpose, and I'm clean and healthy and have hopes for my life. When I first got to prison I remembered going into the chapel and sitting in the back pews, praying, wrestling with guilt and shame and uncertainty. I could hear the battle going on inside my head. The devil was tempting me to be afraid of what people would think, telling me everyone was going to laugh at me and not take me seriously. I remember just finally telling the devil I was done buying into the lies. I acknowledge that the devil is real. I can say that because for far too long I had been consumed with the negative forces that were set out to destroy me. I knew I was on the cusp of a breakthrough because the devil was so adamant about tempting me to step away from praying.

    It was at this moment that my life changed. What started out as me coming into the chapel as an inmate—ashamed, uncertain, and holding my head low in the back of the chapel—turned into me embracing the change that God had revealed for my life. My head was lifted, and I felt an internal encouragement to sit up front with confidence. It was just like sitting in a classroom. I never sat in the back of the room. I always chose to sit up front. That's where I got most out of what was being taught. A new day had come.

I prayed to God and told the devil I was done. I'd rather be wrong about following God than miss out on God's presence. I believe that's the moment when I stood up and left the pews a different man.

The year 2014 finally arrived, and big changes came with it. I had now been incarcerated for three years, and it was amazing looking back on how much had changed for me personally.

I was selected as a participant for the Embark program on the main compound. Along with the Embark program also came a new unit manager for the camp. Can you guess who it was? That's right, it was Mrs. S from the recovery dorm. It turned out that Marion's camp hadn't been state-recognized as a reintegration facility just yet, and she was brought in to make it happen.

A sign-up list was posted; they were looking for guys who were willing to become mentors on the reintegration side of the camp. The mentor would be in charge of handing out accountability charts weekly and collecting them so that they could be documented. According to the requirements of being on the reintegration side, you needed at least forty hours of meaningful activities and programming a week in order to be a participant. I ended up moving over to the reintegration side and became a mentor. I helped guys get into programs and helped them with their paperwork. When new guys came into the dorm, I helped them as well. I was one of several mentors, and it was nice because I knew I was leading by example. At first I faced a few challenges with some of the other guys when it came to filling out the paperwork each week. The differences in opinion were based on how they were used to doing their time. However, the end result was the same; we all wanted to go home.

That spring I was placed on community service and made it out into the community for the first time since being arrested. I was so happy and relieved by it all, because to me it meant I was one step closer to going home. I knew it, I could feel it, I could almost taste it, and I held on to that feeling for inspiration. The community projects would include helping at the city pool before it opened for the summer, helping build shelves in the basement at the local police station, cleaning carpets at the local churches, and even helping out at the local city park, just to name a few things. Some of the guys who did community service with me complained because they didn't want to work, and I just couldn't understand why.

They just didn't want to do anything, and that's when it occurred to me. They didn't have the same vision as me. My desire and my ambitions and visions were different from those of the average guy who was incarcerated. Most were still blind and couldn't see past the fence even when they were actually on the other side of the fence. During the whole time I'd been incarcerated, I'd been looking past the fence. I refused to allow my incarceration to define me, and I felt the same with my recovery. I was able to admit my faults, and it was because of my past actions that I was here. I would not be held down any longer than I had to be by the system.

It had been over two years since having access to the outside of prison. Given the opportunity to leave the facility for community service felt like a privilege. It felt invigorating, followed by a sense of relief to be on the other side of the fence. It was during this time that I came up with the ideas for the two poems I wrote, "33 & 3" and "The Other Side of the Fence." Even though it may sound crazy, the first tree I saw while on community service, I hugged. I refused to accept the bare minimum anymore. I thought to myself, *When I get home I will find ways to better myself. Until I get to a place that is stable and benefits me the most so that I can have a place called home, I will not settle.* This is why I decided to move to Columbus. My hometown did not have the resources and opportunities that I needed to succeed after prison.

33 & 3

Morning dew on the leaves of flowers casts reflections of the morning light onto the honeybees making their programmed rounds. The smell in the air is moist with traces of an earthy combination of dirt, wet tree bark, and fresh-cut grass. A new day has begun, as the crickets die down and the birds begin to sing their songs of flight. Fresh deer tracks speak signs of curiosity to my conscience as they stop at the edge of the backroad that I'm tramping. This opportunity of freedom brings tears of joy to my heart as I truly feel the closeness of You, God, working in my life. Your Glory has impacted my life with great observation. The works You have made in creating this earth can't even compare to spending eternity with You in Your kingdom. You have removed affliction from my life and placed me back on solid ground. My gratitude is as full as all the oceans and flows greater than the greatest waterfall ever imagined. As deep as space I will travel to compare to the void I had in my life before I surrendered to the awesome power of Your love. Thank You, Lord. Thank You for Your refuge. Thank You for Your grace. Thank You for my recovery! In Your eyes I will walk wholeheartedly. As You speak, the heavens clap with thunder, and as You cry You wash away the struggles of this world. You have renewed my purpose. You drive my heart's desire. Your blessings are exceeding abundantly. You are without end. Thank You for prosperity. Today I am clean, I am renewed, I have been made new again.

The Other Side of the Fence

From afar lights on the other side of the fence
remind me of a life I was once familiar with.
Stricken with a past addiction, I live today removed from society.
Dreams of what I look forward to are used as motivation while
two worlds are separated by barbed wire and chain link fence.
The sun sets the same but the air smells different.
The birds are still flying but the grass isn't as green from here.
Most obvious of all is the presence of God!
God's presence is stronger here than it ever was for me on the
other side of the fence, and the men who are the happiest
are the ones doing life!

> As my thoughts subside from the perception of
> what's transpired, the division of two worlds is clear.
> No matter how long my stay in prison, to say I know both
> worlds gives me a deeper appreciation for the quality of life I
> want for myself now, versus the quality of life I once lived,
> On the Other Side of the Fence!

In the following months of doing community service, Mrs. S asked if I would be willing to work outside the fence. It was for a recycling program that was part of the prison called the Green Initiative. She told me the program was getting ready to start, and seven guys were needed for the job. She explained to me that it would be a great opportunity to get forklift experience. Essentially I would be able to use the training to help with getting a job when I came home from prison. I decided to take the opportunity.

It was a dirty job that required digging through trash and separating the recyclables from actual waste. I learned a lot about the different recyclable commodities as we created a staging process. By doing this, it allowed us to track the percentages of our commodities from waste. We were able to separate, weigh, and document our progress daily. It was a great experience, and it also helped my time go by fast. The program gained attention in the community based on the partnership with the surrounding counties. In total, the amount of waste that was recycled showed an average 90 percent diversion rate.

Because of this community initiative that the prison had, the project attracted the attention of the mayor and local media.

Here I was in prison, making the headlines of a local newspaper as a participant in a prison recycling program. I couldn't help but laugh about this. Like I've been saying ever since I got clean, good things continued to happen to me. Turns out all those lies I told myself about being a piece of shit were not true. It was a special moment for me and all of us at the recycling center. I thought to myself I could put another feather in my hat toward focusing on destiny. I knew I was making a difference in my life.

As the Embark program kicked off, we were greeted by volunteers called "navigators." On the first day, we all took turns meeting with each navigator in order to get a feel for one another. Eventually, we were split into groups of three as we began the first of the two classes. My navigator's name was Tom. The class was called Celebrate Recovery, which was the twelve-step program based on biblical principles. As I described earlier, the program was set up in a way that we were able to read and share in small groups, and then in those individual groups, we would meet again on the next scheduled date to go over the work. The other class that Embark provided was Getting it Right. This is the course that has been categorized as a cognitive behavioral therapy program. This program was great because it helped you navigate through certain issues more successfully.

As things continued to progress with my programming and work, so did the title "Reintegration" at Marion's Correctional Camp. That same year, Mrs. S told us that the state was coming in to sign off on classifying Marion's camp as a state-recognized reintegration facility. She asked me if I would prepare a five-minute speech and said that I was one of a few individuals she had selected to speak. The day of the ribbon-cutting ceremony was busy and exciting. Not only for the camp but for me as well. The last time I had had this much attention on me was when I got arrested.

There I was, three and a half years clean, speaking on behalf of Marion's newly certified reintegration center and how it had contributed to my personal development. I can't forget to mention that the director of the State of Ohio's prison system, Gary Mohr, was there. That's a heck of an accomplishment considering everything I'd been through. Not to mention how far I'd come personally in such a short amount of time. Through all the programs I was involved in, one of the best things that Marion Correctional offered was a band room. That's right; a band room. Drums, speakers, keyboards, and microphones. Anything and everything you could think of that would be needed to start a band, Marion had it.

With that being said, I was in a band with a few guys out at the camp. All our music was original, and I was the lead singer. Even though I loved singing, it wasn't anything I could write home about, but it did help me with my writing. The name of our band was Emersion. I liked the word, which I was drawn to during a Bible study one afternoon. What caught my attention, though, was when I realized *immersion* and *emersion* shared the root word *emerge*, which also means "to rise above." Most importantly, it's why I decided to go with *emersion* for the title of my book. The definition was a beautiful description of my life.

I appreciated both words and felt that they were relevant to my life and relatable too. This is also how the band name came to be. I wasn't the only singer and writer; the other lead was Kyle. This guy had such amazing talent. He could listen to a song and figure it out on the guitar without reading any music notes. He could also write lyrics, and most importantly he had a hell of a voice. Kyle sounded just like Layne Staley from Alice in Chains.

I met Kyle after he transferred from another prison. We hit it off fairly quickly because of his personality. His sense of humor was kiddish, which at times took the focus off the fact that we were in prison. As I continued to help as a mentor on the reintegration side and as a sponsor in recovery, my routine schedule was full. My average week of meaningful time consisted of sixty hours Monday to Friday. I was pretty busy, and it wasn't expected, but our friendship just happened naturally. With everything going on through work and classes, my time did go fast.

I never thought I would be able to say it, but prison started to feel like a normal routine. Especially with being in a band now. February 2015 started the new year with new opportunities. Well, that's what I thought, except everything changed without warning. One morning, while working at the recycling center, I was driving the forklift and taking pallets outside to move boxes around. I came back in, and everyone was standing in a single-file line staring at two other men I had never seen before. One of the two guys speaking to the group turned around, and I saw he had a badge.

He told me with an elevated stern voice to stop, "Get off the lift and don't move!" As he was walking up to me, he reached behind his back and grabbed a pair of handcuffs. I asked what was going on and he stated, "You'll find out soon enough." After being detained with the rest of the group, each and every one of us was taken around the corner to another room in the building and strip-searched. I was thinking to myself, *What the hell is going on?* Obviously something had happened, but I still didn't know what. Once everyone was searched, the two men walked the whole group back to the compound and placed us in the hole.

I was mind-blown by the sequence of events that had just taken place. I thought that there had to be some kind of mistake. My entire time in prison has been fairly straightforward. I hadn't been in any fights or any trouble.

The hole was a section of the prison that was like a giant closet.

I had heard stories about it but had never been there until now. You went through a double set of doors, and each one had to be unlocked by a guard electronically in a security office. Once you got through both doors, the hole was this dark, horseshoe-shaped, two-story, hall-looking dungeon. It was dark and dreary and cold. Each cell was a solid door. Not like you see on TV where it's a bunch of cells with bars. No, these were closed cells, much like the ones from Lorain.

Once I got to my cell and the door was shut behind me, that was it. I was given bed sheets, toilet paper, toothpaste, a toothbrush, and a Styrofoam cup to use for water out of the sink. No answers to why I was in the hole or anything. None of the guys who had been with me on the walk over seemed to know anything when we were escorted back. While in the hole, each time the officer made their rounds, I would ask if I could talk to the investigator. In return, the guard just said they were working on it.

What did that even mean? Over the course of two days, I was able to get a Bible, a pencil, and a notepad upon request from the guards. Eventually, I gave up asking for anything else. If you remember back when I first explained how my cell in Lorain was, well, Marion was worse in comparison to those conditions.

No exaggeration. Old, cracked glass windows with frozen brick walls in the month of February. Snow was coming through the windows, with extremely dim lighting in the cell. It felt like a maximum-security psych ward. Now that I think of it, when I was in Lorain, it was during the month of February as well. I have no idea about the correlation to that, but it is odd to think about it.

The only thing I knew to do was write, read my Bible, do push-ups, and try to meditate. I dug deep within myself, trying to meditate and focus on God. I kept asking God to give me an understanding of why this was happening. I had been in the hole for a week, and one evening, while I was reading the Bible, a group of guys from the chapel showed up. They were going from cell to cell, reaching out to anyone willing to listen. Turned out, through the chapel, the chaplain and warden had allowed a ministry group of other inmates to be escorted by a guard to come into the hole and talk to the guys.

I knew the group of guys very well, and we began to talk. One brother said, "Take this time not to focus on why you are here but focus on what God is showing you.... Keep reading," he told me. At that point, I still had no answers. It was like I had been erased from the general population. I was a hostage, it felt like. I got to the point while reading the Bible where I would just flip pages and stop.

On that particular day, I came across Matthew 21:33-45, the parable of the Evil Farmers. This applied to me because God was the farmer, and he left the work to his people. In the end, some of those people abused the vineyard, which in my life at the time was the recycling center. The people involved did evil by it and were struck by God. Being in the hole wasn't about me so much, but it affected me. I knew I hadn't done anything wrong.

My hunches told me that somebody had done something wrong or had tried to escape or something like that. I still wasn't sure what it was, but I was caught in the midst of it. I knew that God would prevail in my life, though. The hole was a dark place for a lot of men. At times, it sounded like an insane asylum. Guys banging on the doors, screaming and laughing out loud with insanity. I had never experienced anything like it.

You could hear the torment in this place. All through the night, you could hear screaming as if someone was being tortured. At one point during my time in the hole on the second floor, someone clogged the toilet and flooded their cell. I began to think of the history behind this prison. A dark and sadistic side emerged as I thought back on the history of the prison. I began to think about the skeletons that this place hid inside its walls. I could feel the energy and the fear along with isolation from the other prisoners.

The hole reminded me of an old, wet, damp basement. I could smell the old steel bars on the windows. The old metal door reminded me of a dungeon, where you're locked away, never to be released. I knew this was a test of faith, but at the same time I felt that I was being tasked with more. That second week, I was finally called into the investigator's office. This is where I was met by an Ohio state patrol investigator. There I was, interrogated and accused of being involved in the conveyance of drugs and cell phones. I told the cop he had already predetermined his opinion of me based on the fact that I was in prison and my past charges.

I told him, "Nowhere in that folder do you have my accomplishments or the fact that I have years of recovery. Not to mention my involvement in the prison community. You're wrong about me. I suggest you look a little deeper into how much I have changed versus how much you think I had a part in this." After the investigation was over, I was taken back to the hole. I was relieved in a sense that I had been able to speak up for myself. The investigation was tense as I was subjected to accusations and a lot of mind games.

What else could I do? I truly didn't know what had happened out there. I thought to myself, *Whoever was a part of bringing drugs and phones into prison should just step up and accept what they did. Why bring a whole group of people down who didn't have anything to do with it? If you're guilty, you're guilty. Own up to it and accept the consequences.* Back to the cell I went.

I lay there in that cold, dark room and reflected on my entire life. My childhood. The decisions I had made while in Pittsburgh with heroin. The people I had affected because of my addiction. I also thought about how far I had come in my recovery. I knew there was more to life than where I was at this particular moment. I thought to myself, *This is just a minor setback. At least I'm not doing a life sentence.*

I was innocent, and regardless of the outcome, I wasn't going to allow this situation to stifle my journey to healing. My time in the hole took two whole weeks before I was finally released and returned to the camp. On my way back out at the camp, I was greeted by guys in passing. Everyone out there whom I knew told me they were certain I was innocent. While I was unpacking everything, even the corrections officer talked to me. He told me he had no doubts that I would be back out at the camp. I felt vindicated and relieved, but at the same time I couldn't unsee my experience in isolation. It was stressful and mind-opening to the fact that there were guys in the hole seriously struggling with mental health issues from the isolation.

At the same time, though, I knew there were guys in the hole who needed to be there. Guys like the foot smeller I dealt with when I first got to prison. Guys who came from other prisons who couldn't adjust to the new facility. After all, there are people in prison who have done horrible things to other people. Even while in prison, people continue to do heinous things to others. The hole has its place in every institution. I, for one, was just glad to put its existence behind me. Back at the camp, I was given a single rack again. I was in a better location than before, but I didn't have my neighbor, Brother Maine.

The bed I had now faced a large bay window that overlooked a field with a pond in the distance. Every evening, I was able to watch the sun set. It allowed me to get away from the barriers that so many men were failing to escape. Every evening, I would reflect on the view I had and imagine a life without limitations, just openness. For me, that sunset was a motivation for the new life I was working toward once released. As I unpacked my belongings, I found that nothing was missing, which was a relief. My deepest concern was about my writings and certificates of completion that I intended to send to the judge.

Usually, when guys get packed up, they come to find that things were stolen or misplaced once they return from the hole. I was glad to find that everything was still intact. *Grateful* was an understatement. I came out of that ordeal with a new outlook on how I was going to do the rest of my time. The torment inside that facility gave me a deeper appreciation for God's presence in my life. The men who were still in the hole were a reminder of my soul during my years of addiction. I never wanted that life again and was willing to do whatever it took to never return to that pain. The pain and trauma I had in my past were based on my childhood and addiction. Something I was able to pinpoint very early on. However, there are many people in the world who still struggle with holding on to pain, which keeps them tied to their addictions and trauma.

The fact that my father wasn't around when I was a child changed me. My stepfather was extremely abusive to me and my mother. Because of it, I carried a lot of uncertainty and doubt toward ever being worthy of anything good as I got older. Turned out, the unresolved issues behind all that pain were never properly addressed. This, in turn, led to my issues with self-doubt and acceptance. The older I got, my decision-making around drugs and alcohol became an obsessive compulsion. I ended up embracing it rather than turning it down. The analogy to my addiction was compared to that of a bug bite or poison ivy. Even though scratching felt good, it didn't help, because the more you scratched it, the longer it took to heal. The only difference for me was that the infected area that I wanted to itch was my whole life. My addiction went far deeper than the surface of my skin. It was going to take longer to heal.

There were years of pain and turmoil that I lived with from the abuse of my stepfather, Bob, and the absence of my biological father. With all that, it still could never compare to the abuse my mother endured. I can recall many nights as a child being woken up to the sound of slamming doors and glass breaking as my stepfather would beat on my mom and throw things at her. I would lie in my room, helpless and in fear because of his rage. I remember wishing he were dead or that he would just disappear. I often recalled seeing bruising on my mom's forearms as a child. Purple, green, and blue were the familiar shades that we both shared.

Mine were always on my legs and lower back, which made it painful to sit down. I struggled with behavioral issues at school because of it. Then he would beat me for it when the school called the house. One painful memory was when I was awakened in the middle of the night by a vicious smack across the face. There was a flash of bright light as I felt the contact of his hand on my face. He was drunk again. I could smell it on his breath.

The pain was excruciating, and all I could hear was a loud ringing in my ear. My natural reaction was to curl up in a ball and turn my back to him as I anticipated more lashings. Instead, I remember him rambling on about something I didn't understand at the time. He said, "You will never be better than me." Then he just got up and left the house. He was doing to me and my mother what had been done to him. It wasn't right, but for whatever reason, he felt it to be necessary. I was around seven years old at that time.

Fast-forward twenty-five-plus years. I'm in prison and on the phone with my mom as she's telling me Bob had died. He'd died from a massive heart attack. As I was talking to my mom, I prayed for Bob's soul. I told God, I don't have much to say about this man, and I know You know what our family went through. God, I pray that he is at peace now. I wouldn't call it closure, but there was a sense of relief in my mom's voice as I prayed with her on the phone. I was relieved, but when it came to my mom, she was the one who had lived in fear the most. She not only suffered from the fear of getting beaten by Bob, but the fear of having to protect her children.

The Hole

Dark and cold I'm all alone,
Placed in a cell they call the hole.
Locked up why? I haven't a clue!
Surrounded by darkness, what would you do?
I question my self-worth and all my hard work.
I even wondered, how is this justice at work?
I went to God, thanking Him for all that I've got.
In scripture, it says, Question me not!
I got on my knees and cried with humility,
Please God Please…! Truly I'm sorry.
At first, I thought this was punishment!
But now I see its spiritual strength.
At times I'm weak, but God keeps me strong.
He picks me up to carry me along.
My past doesn't define who I am today.
It's built me up so I'm not led astray.

My new neighbor was a guy I knew from over the years of being out at the camp. Todd was my workout partner. The guy was built like a Viking. I looked up to him as an older brother as well as a mentor. He was always filled with good advice and was an all-around good listener when I talked to him. Todd's experiences and growth while doing his time helped me during my prison term. Looking at challenges or ideas through a different lens is always a good approach. He helped me to use critical thinking before making any decisions. That's exactly how Todd and I connected, through meaningful conversation. He was always there to bounce ideas off, and he was supportive of my spiritual growth as well.

To this day, I am still in contact with Todd, and even though he is still in prison, our relationship continues to grow. He is my brother through Christ. It wasn't until I was getting ready to leave that he told me he was doing a life sentence. I would never have known if he had not shared that with me. Todd has been incarcerated since 1986. Without going into too many details out of respect for him and his case specifics, he was nineteen when he was incarcerated. Todd's approach to being better every day and always learning something new has helped shape me to find the confidence within myself. The moral of Todd's story—and of so many of the other guys doing life—is that it's never too late to change and to make a difference in our own lives. You never know how those decisions are going to affect someone else later on in life.

When I first got to the camp, I had signed up for a weekend Bible retreat called Kairos. It took me over a year to get accepted to the program, but when I did, I can tell you the experience was gratifying. You had to apply and go through an interview process to be selected for Kairos. Kairos is an international program geared toward deepening one's faith, identity, and relationship with God. This retreat lasts three days and is filled with individual testimonies and activities that allow you to reflect on your relationship with God. The Kairos program comes around twice a year and allows you to connect with a community of other participants, volunteers, and graduates. Oh, and I can't forget the cookies, coffee, and food.

The word *Kairo* is special, coming from the Greek language. Kairos means "God's timing," and that's exactly how this program came into my life. After graduating from the weekend retreat, every so often, there would be a reunion. This allowed graduates to come together and catch up, sharing with one another new testimonies of how God was still working in our lives. The motto we went by during the group activities was "Listen, listen, love, love."

Kindway Embark, the ministry program that my friend Jordan told me to get involved with, is structured in the same way. When it comes to Kindway Embark reunions, the get-togethers are held both while in prison and once you're released. For more information on the Kindway program or how to get involved, please visit www.kindway.org. While in prison, the reunions are exceptionally nice. It allows for fellowship and conversation that takes you away from the focus of your incarceration. What I mean is that even though you never really lose sight of the fact that you're incarcerated, the reunions provide an opportunity to leave your dorm or cell to spend time with volunteers in the chapel.

The chapel was neutral ground and respected by everyone in prison. The gang stuff and violence were left at the doors. Chapel was a place to reflect. With the reunions, it was humbling to meet and know the volunteers who took time out of their personal lives to come in. Devoting their time to helping the men and women grow and prepare for a successful release is a true definition of selflessness. To me, these reunions were vital and at times more important than some of the classes I took. They allowed me to break away from everything else and feel normal in a not-so-normal element. It's a strange concept, but while meeting with everyone during the reunions, I would envision my life after incarceration.

Now I'm not sure if things have changed since Covid, but while I was incarcerated, every time Kairos came to the institution, so did the cookies. The unique thing about the cookies was that the outside volunteers would spend a lot of time baking the cookies at their local churches. Every individual in the whole prison, including the selected group of Kairos participants, received two dozen cookies. Literally, each person received a Ziploc bag with two dozen cookies in it. The cookies were intended to be used as a peace offering to someone you may have had an unresolved issue with before receiving the cookies. In prison, the cookies were dubbed "forgiveness cookies."

The distribution of these cookies was a big event among the institution. It was interesting to watch these grown men get excited to the point where even the toughest guys would smile. It was because of programs such as this that I was able to connect with men like Todd. To this day, there is a list of men in my life that I still write to in prison. They played an integral part in my growth while incarcerated. Ultimately, it's the testimonies of how God transformed each of their lives that make experiences like mine worthy to write about. God's timing was no coincidence in my life. His presence has shone through each leg of my journey. I believe that ever since that day in August 2011 when I prayed to God for help, he has shown up and delivered a hundredfold.

Todd was always finding ways to take more classes and learn something new. I respected his approach to how he was doing his time. It taught me how to stay focused on self-development. The last year of prison for me was anything but routine. The last few months were daunting while I awaited the response from the lawyer about my release. Todd helped me with that by sharing his outlook on the whole situation. He told me the worst-case scenario was the result that I already knew. Whatever amount of time I had to serve was what was to come if I got denied.

"You're going home at some point" is what he told me. As for Todd, all he had to go off of was the next time he was expected to meet with the parole board. If he was denied, he still knew he had a life sentence. That insight humbled me, and I needed that because it brought me back to reality. I couldn't imagine having a life sentence. The amazing thing I thought about was how men like Todd carried themselves in prison and the commonality that they all had: their relationship with God.

My lawyer filed for my judicial review in July, and it could have taken until October to find out if I was going home. During that time, I continued with my scheduled routine. One day in September, I got a very sad letter. Amelia and Mia's mother wrote to inform me that Mia had succumbed to her addiction. It was gut-wrenching to say the least. I was hopeful that one day I would be able to at least see her clean, whether it be in person or through social media. I at least wanted to say "Hi" and possibly be some sort of motivation.

I sat on my bed and started crying before I could finish reading the letter after the horrible news. It's tragic living the life of a heroin addict. You either end up dying or going to prison or both.

There is no other outcome. I'm a blessing, just like so many others who have quit using. It doesn't make it any easier, though. You survive, but you have to watch everyone who can't figure it out suffer and die. That letter sucked and it hurt to read. Letters like that can't be unread; they're gut-wrenching.

It wasn't only Mia who passed away that year. There was a well-known guy by the name of Spanky at Marion. He had fourteen prison numbers over twenty-two years. That didn't include jail, and it didn't include the times he came back to prison on an old prison number. Yes, you can leave prison and come back on the same number. Let's say you get out of prison and have a parole violation. The court system sends you back to the same previous number. Spanky was a career offender. Institutionalized, to say it politely. He was my sponsor Terry's uncle. Well, Spanky got out and decided to relapse, and he died two weeks after getting out. Yes, 2015 was a crazy year.

For ninety days, I waited to hear from my lawyer about a court date. When I did, the news came by way of legal mail. I was so excited and happy that I could barely contain myself. My whole time at Marion was coming to an end, and this was exactly what I had prepared for. After the challenges and unexpected situations I had been through, my time for release had finally arrived. All the personal growth I had gained and every hardship I had endured, I was finally able to timeline it all. I walked back to the camp and immediately called home to share the news with my mom. Everything I had anticipated and prepared for had finally come to light. I told a few guys I was close to, like Todd and Brother Maine, but other than that, I just didn't share that information.

In my opinion, your most vulnerable time in prison is when you first get to prison and right before you leave. Let me explain. When you first come to prison, everyone in your housing unit knows it, and at some point or another, you're going to be tested. It's just part of the process. Every institution is different, and I've heard horror stories from people getting jumped as soon as they get into their dorm. Mostly for reasons related to gangs, race, or even sex crimes. When situations like this happen, you stand your ground and fight, whether you win or lose. If it's gang-related, most of the time the fighting is to get the new person to "check in" or leave the dorm.

Other reasons are for extortion and punishment for being a sex offender. When you get close to going home, though, you're just as vulnerable, in my opinion. People don't care about your time. Some inmates have longer sentences and don't care if you're going home. They will intentionally try and cause you to have more time. It's called "crashing out," and I've seen it happen before. Sometimes people will crash out on their own, either to get to the hole until it's time to be released, or they crumble under pressure. Ultimately, they end up getting more time because they ruin their chances of an early release for fighting. This is why I never shared my information with anyone.

Everything I had worked on and prepared for was about to take effect. It was time to sink or swim. Society doesn't care whether you make it or not. It's completely up to you what you do with your life after you're released. I started reevaluating all my ideas and the potential job leads I had come up with over the years. I thought about what leads I could use once I got to Columbus. Finally, one night in October, the guard came up to me and told me to pack it up. She said to be ready to head downstairs at four a.m. It was now around nine p.m., and I started to give everything away except my hygiene, underwear, socks, legal paperwork, and literature.

My life felt different, and I hadn't even left yet. Being told you're going home changes you. I had a hard time falling asleep that night. I just kept thinking of my life over the previous four years. I thought about all the people who have died over the years. I thought about the people who weren't going home yet. I thought about the men who had life sentences; specifically, the ones who had helped me over the last four years. I was already beginning to miss them. Saying it was bittersweet was an understatement.

I thought about everything I had experienced during my incarceration. The growth personally and with family. The involvement I had out at the reintegration center as a mentor. My years of recovery and sponsoring others, and my newfound relationship with God. My time at Marion Correctional had been transformative on so many different levels.

I thought to myself, no more standing in line for bags of partially expired milk for breakfast. No more ground-up chicken that had fragments of bone still in it. The chicken cubes were the worst, but you still ate them because you were hungry. It had a texture that reminded me of chewing on an eraser. No more standing in line waiting for food with the other several hundred men, only to watch a group of young guys skip the whole line because they were hungrier than everyone else. No more waiting to use the phone. No more shower shoes and taking a shower with other men at the same time.

No more count time. No more hoping for visits. No more commissary. No more strip searches. No more three a.m. drug tests. No more standing in line waiting to use the toilet after breakfast because the food didn't sit right in your stomach. These things were just the tip of the iceberg. Nonetheless, God showed up each step of the way. The closer to understanding the power of God, the more I began to realize how powerful I truly was through my faith in Him alone.

Despite the fact that I had felonies on my record, it didn't matter, because I was clean, and I was getting out of prison. Everything I had prayed for and truly believed with every ounce of my being was beginning to manifest right in front of me. The biblical analogy "Faith of a mustard seed can move a mountain" speaks volumes to me, and I understand it now. We have to pray without ceasing, with full conviction that someday our prayers will be answered. This conviction of faith can manifest our deepest desires. The most important thing that I have been able to gather from this newfound belief system is that the outcome of our desires is God's timing, not ours. Our prayers could be answered right this very second, or it could be years down the road, but the power is ours to imagine something greater for ourselves.

During my addiction, before I knew the magnitude of my thoughts, I believed I would get clean. At the same time, I also feared I would die from my drug use. It was a living nightmare. I always had a deep belief that there was a greater purpose for my life, and I never lost sight of that.

Finally, four a.m. came around, and I was ready to go. The corrections officer went through and documented every article of clothing and belonging I had, because I couldn't take it with me. I was going to need a family member to come back and pick it up. Technically, I wasn't being released from prison. I was going back to court.

It's a policy that every institution has, but I didn't care. I was ready to leave. By nine a.m. I was loaded up by two sheriffs and taken back to the county jail. The drive back felt different. Everything seemed brighter, and the drive was shorter than I had once remembered. As soon as I got back to the county jail, I was put back in the same dorm where I had originally started my time. I walked into the dorm and saw my old bed and thought of all the guys I had known back then.

None of those guys were there anymore. There was a whole new cycle of men, and every bed was filled. It was disheartening to think about. I knew some of the men were there for a short time, and some of them were waiting to go to prison. The one thing that stood out to me was that the majority of the guys were younger, not only by appearance but by maturity. I remembered years earlier that my time in county jail seemed to be quieter, but now there was an energy in the dorm that felt more chaotic. I stayed to myself and observed my surroundings. I focused on what was to come and tried not to get distracted from that.

A few kids talked to me, and I was able to share my story with the ones who had asked about prison. I can't say whether it impacted them or not, but I felt God was able to use me in that moment, and that was all that mattered. My stay in the county took two weeks before I transitioned over to the CBCF (Community-Based Correctional Facility). The CBCF was the last part of my judicial release. It was court-ordered that I go through the transitional program. Oddly enough, the CBCF was directly across the street from the county jail.

As I was being processed at intake, I could hear guys on the other side of the door laughing and carrying on with one another. I heard an unmistakable laugh that made me think, *I know that laugh.* Sure enough, I got into the main area of the facility and it was Big Country. Arms wide open with huge smiles, we walked toward each other and gave one another a long-overdue hug. After four long years, we saw each other again. He looked healthy and happy, and between the two of us, there wasn't enough time in the day to catch up.

He told me that after he wrote me from prison, he came home and got back into using. He was at his parents' house one evening, and his dad called the cops on him again. He was arrested, and that's how he ended up back in jail. It was not a healthy relationship between him and his father. There were times when his father would let him come over and stay. Then there were times when his father would let him come over and they would get high together. His father would then threaten to call the cops on him. He went on to explain how he spent the last six months or so in and out of county jail. Eventually, the courts sent him to CBCF as an alternative to prison.

Thinking back on everything we have been through in life, I just can't believe the timeline of events. How do we go from kids to young adults addicted to drugs and ending up in jail and prison? I'm reminded of all the memories we had, and it's hard not to think of what life was going to be like for us after this. The majority of the people in this facility didn't really take this program seriously. I couldn't fault them; I was once in the same mindset. The way I looked at it, they hadn't really hit their rock bottom yet. They hadn't experienced enough hardship yet. Over the years, what I've come to find out is that most people who do end up in prison still don't change. It's not for me to judge; it's just my observation.

There were a lot of distractions, from finally being out of county jail and then running into Big Country. The one thing I couldn't lose sight of, though, was being able to come home and see my mom. Once I called my mom and told her I was at the transitional facility, she was very excited. The very next day, she dropped off bed sheets, a real pillow, and other personal belongings. I was also allowed to have laundry soap and wash my sheets and clothes again. I got my wallet back, and I was allowed to carry cash again. The best part was that eventually I was going to be allowed to go out and find a temporary job. All this was a wonderful feeling. Oddly enough, though, when I began to unpack my belongings, a lot of my old outfits reminded me of my past. The outfits were a time capsule of my past life and no longer fit my personality.

The first dorm I moved into was not good. My one roommate had sleep apnea so bad that his snoring made it impossible to sleep. He was about six feet tall and pushing four hundred pounds, and it was the worst snoring I had ever experienced in my life. The dorm room was a ten-by-twelve-foot room with two bunk beds in it. His snoring seemed to create an echo chamber that could be heard from the next room over. The snoring was one issue, but his feet made it even more unbearable. The smelly feet and the guy's snoring got the room dubbed "the Swamp."

It was my third day at the facility, and one of the guys asked me how the Swamp was working out. I said, "The Swamp?" He laughed and replied, "Yeah, your roommate Murph. We call him the Swamp Monster." I knew I had to get out. I told the guy I didn't have any problems with him; I just couldn't sleep. He was a great guy, and I got along with him well. His sense of humor reminded me of the late Chris Farley. With all things aside, I had to switch rooms, though. Years later, unfortunately, I found out Murph overdosed on heroin a year after his release. News like this is always unexpected and sad. It stops you in your tracks.

When I get news like this, it's hard for me not to go through the list of people I've come to know over the years. It's a stark reminder of just how thin a line is that we walk every day. You never know when your time on earth is going to be over. I always pray for people's souls because I never know where they are spiritually. There was another person I knew who passed away who happened to be another roommate of mine at the CBCF. Only this time, I was still in the facility when everyone found out. He didn't make it two weeks after he left the facility because of a heroin overdose.

He left behind his family and his son. It's frustrating because I knew why he relapsed. I lived the same life for almost ten years. I don't know how I made it through my twenties. I started thinking about how that news would have affected my family and friends if it were me. The class talked about his passing, and I shared my feelings and thoughts.

I said it's strange when someone passes who you knew. They are no longer with us now, and yet our lives continue. I think about whether we are able to talk with those individuals after they have passed. What advice would they give us? Then you think,

Was it worth picking up again? Knowing they can see the pain that has been left upon their loved ones, would they say it was worth it or not? I doubt it. I know they would want to take that last choice back.

The classes were all the same for me from when I was in prison, so my approach was the same. I continued to give 110 percent to working on myself. Even though the classes were the same, it was different being in them, because most of these men had never been to prison. They hadn't had the reality of doing time and being stripped of everything. Your life is reduced to what you can fit into a 12-by-24-inch box and a bed. They weren't seeing it from my perspective.

I'm not sure how much of an impact my sharing made while in the group. Opening up helped me decompress, and I shared how I felt about transitioning after years of incarceration. I shared everything I was feeling, from the realization of coming home to even describing how it felt to wear normal clothes again. Coming to the CBCF came with a whole new list of responsibilities, including doing my laundry again. I never realized how doing laundry and using fabric softener and dryer sheets could be so therapeutic. It was a weird idea, but it was something I was happy to be doing again.

One of the more serious topics that I shared in the group was the concept behind finding a job for the first time again. It was overwhelming and stressful. I prepared how I was going to articulate the fact that I just got out of prison. The challenge lay with actually explaining it in person. As simple as it seems, it was overwhelming to explain your employment gaps on your resume. You also have to properly articulate the felonies on your record.

Thankfully, with Big County being there, he was able to help me by being a reference. Big Country started working at Bob Evans as a cook and was loving it. I mean, who wouldn't? Especially after being locked up and eating prison food for all those years. It was a match made in heaven at that point. He told me he put in a good word to the manager, and they wanted to meet me when I was able to leave the facility for a job.

I had to stay in the facility for Thanksgiving and Christmas that year because I'd missed the deadline. I was so close to coming home, and I was looking forward to spending time with my family again. Most of the guys were gone on their home passes, and my arrival into the facility was too late. When it was my turn to start looking for a job, my first interview was naturally with Bob Evans. I left the same day with the job as a cook.

My first actual job in over four years felt great to me. The cool thing about meeting this manager was that he already had a general idea about my current situation. The manager, John, was a very laid-back guy. At the end of the interview, he reassured me that he thought I was going to do great. I looked him in the eye, shook his hand, and thanked him for the job.

He emphasized that he believed in second chances and also stated that I could work all the hours I wanted. He even gave me a free meal. Naturally, I went with the turkey dinner. It was my first real meal since 2011. The turkey and gravy with green beans and mashed potatoes were steaming off the plate. As I sat in the corner of the restaurant and looked out the window, I noticed there were no fences with barbed wire. Just an open field with snow as the sun started to set for the evening. I had missed Thanksgiving and Christmas with my family, yet the meal made up for it in a strange way. I prayed over my food and said, "God, thank You. You have blessed me beyond measure. This is just the beginning, and I'm truly grateful for Your grace. Thank You for saving my life."

That same week, my mother came and picked me up and took me to the store for hygiene products. It was a two-hour pass, so we went to Walmart. Being with my mother for the first time alone in public was special. I probably told her I loved her a hundred times. I'm sure I apologized to her ten times more. It was so strange to finally be in a car again. The feeling of not having her see me in handcuffs or a prison uniform was gratifying.

The excitement of being with my mother outside of prison for the first time was truly humbling. I cried when I first hugged her, and we talked about everything, including family. During all the years I had been gone, one of my deepest wishes was for my grandmother to stay alive to see me clean and released from prison. My grandmother had been through so much in her later years. She had survived colon cancer and heart surgery. I was looking forward to seeing her in the next couple of months.

My mother has been my number one advocate and supporter from the beginning—visiting me in jail, driving to see me in prison, providing me with money, even getting my certificates to the lawyer for my judicial release. She was and always will be my deepest and greatest supporter. Even though the Walmart experience was wonderful, it was overwhelming. Being in that store, I realized all the things I had taken for granted before prison opened my mind.

When it comes to food and hygiene in prison, everything is fairly basic, and you're not faced with so many options and decisions in the commissary. Walmart's selections seemed endless, and I felt like I had to relearn how to shop again.

It's amazing how you forget all the options you have in life. It's only after you're incarcerated that you begin to think about those amenities you had taken for granted. While in prison, I recalled looking in the newspaper flyers around the holidays and reading the grocery store coupons. I would imagine making holiday meals again and thinking about old family recipes. On the way back to CBCF, my mom told me she had the phone number and mailing address for Kindway Embark while I was in prison.

At this point in time, I was preparing for a transfer to Columbus, and my mom helped me get in touch with the prison ministry program. I needed this because I had to request a letter of support from them. I had to present that to my parole officer before the transfer could be approved. Not only did incarceration save my life, but it has also brought me closer to my mother. Our relationship is better than it has ever been, and I couldn't be more grateful. The level of respect and trust that we have for each other now is indescribable.

While I was incarcerated, Big Country would stop and check in on my mom from time to time, when he wasn't in trouble. Every now and again, when I would call home from prison, she would tell me he had stopped by to say hello. That was a good feeling because he was the only one out of everyone I knew who did that. I had so many people upset with me over the years because of my involvement with heroin. I became the scapegoat for how heroin came to town. People on social media posted on my page calling me a crackhead and everything else you could think of. I wrestled with that for several years and struggled with worrying about what everyone thought of me.

It was during my incarceration that I worked through the twelve steps and other developmental programs, finally addressing the underlying issues. I was a people pleaser, and through that, I felt the need for others' approval. I worried so much about being compared to and/or accepted that I allowed myself to carry those burdens on my back. Once I was able to address that, I was able to move on from a lot of my past. Big Country at least took the time to visit my mother despite how messed up his own life was. That meant the world to me.

Here I was now preparing for release from CBCF, and as my mom was dropping me off, she saw Big Country on his way to work. It was nice because, as you know, we had grown up together. Big Country, with his smile, laughingly said, "HI, Linda." My mom smiled back and said, "I hope you've learned your lesson this time." He jokingly said, "Oh, you know me, Linda." My mom raised her fist and shook it at him, suggesting a knuckle sandwich. That evening, after Big Country came back from work, we sat at the cafeteria table and drank coffee and just talked.

I shared with him my concerns about coming home and how I needed to start fresh. Even though I have moved on in life, there will always be remorse for my past. I know I caused a lot of pain for many families through my heroin addiction. Not only did I contribute, but I participated like so many others did by picking up the drug for the first time. Unfortunately, many people have died because of that choice. I can't explain why I'm still here and never overdosed. All I know is that today I have a chance to live right and share my story. Hopefully, those who are struggling can find motivation to stop using and change their lives before it's too late.

While Big Country and I were talking, I told him who my parole officer was. He said that the guy was cool. He had the same officer before for supervision. I was excited about my release, and he could see it. He told me to get the hell out of town and patted me on the back. We talked about life and reminisced over memories of growing up.

We talked about Cody and even joked about how he would ride around town with his moped popping wheelies. Cody could ride a wheelie on just about any two-wheeled vehicle he got his hands on. One night, when we were kids, Cody stole his dad's Honda Gold Wing motorcycle and got caught by the police. That was a whole ordeal that didn't end well for him. When he brought Cody home, the officer told his parents they had caught him doing wheelies. We sounded like two kids laughing that night while catching up. It was a nice memory to have because we were clean and healthy.

I finally started working at Bob Evans, and it was great. I often worked nights and took classes during the day. Eventually, I started working mornings on the weekends to help with the breakfast rush. Big Country completed CBCF one morning, and we had our last cup of coffee together outside. It was a cold February morning in Ohio. The sky was clear and layered with several shades of blue, orange, and yellow. As the sun began to rise over the horizon, we talked while he smoked his cigarette. I told him, "I need to talk to you about something. I'm sorry for offering you heroin."

With his head down, staring at the steam coming from his cup of coffee, he turned and looked me straight in the face with an expression I'd never seen from him before. It was almost as if he wanted to cry. He said, "You don't have to apologize, man. It was my choice. I know you've carried a lot of pain since Cody passed away. I forgive you. None of us thought our lives would end up this way."

The feeling was so intense, I wanted to cry. I could feel his pain because it was real for me as well. I've lost so many people close to me over the years; it was hard to describe how it felt. Hearing this meant more than I could ever explain. The fact that he thought about it was immensely valuable. For years, I carried this burden within and internalized it greatly. Living with the burden of losing someone that you were close to is a pain that never goes away.

You're haunted by it. Their memory is a recurring thought that appears every time you see or do something that reminds you of them. Since I've been clean, being able to deal with my thoughts and emotions has been extremely hard. It gets emotional at times because you're forced to process your thoughts and feelings. That day in February was one of the best memories I ever had with Big Country. He completed the program and was officially a free man with another chance to do things differently. I was proud of him, and I made sure to let him know that.

I wasn't able to watch him leave the facility that morning because I had class. However, I got to work with him that night. At work, he showed me pictures of his new place and told me he was going to start looking for a better-paying job now that he had more time. The following week, I received my letter of support from Embark and got the approval from my parole officer. The officer explained to me that he would get the process started, and it should be ready by the time I graduated from the program.

That weekend I helped open Bob Evans for breakfast, and Big Country was supposed to be there, and he was late. He eventually showed up two hours later, and I could tell something wasn't right. He had started drinking again and I made sure I had a chance to talk to him about it. I told him, "You need to stay clean. You need to keep working the program, or else eventually you're going to end up back in the same situation. You need to give yourself time, you just got out." I reminded him of how hard he had worked to get out of everything. At first, he got mad at me and told me not to judge him. I understood why he felt that way because he was being confronted with something he knew deep down wasn't right.

I told him, "I'm not judging you. I'm holding you accountable for your actions. As a friend, would you rather I not say anything at all? I can't just sit back and do that. It's not who I am today, and I want to see you reach your full potential." He never really responded to the question, and I have to admit it was awkward but worth it. I explained to him that I didn't think any less of him. I just didn't want to see anything bad happen, and the conversation was left at that.

The following week, my counselor pulled me into the office and explained to me that there had been a mix-up in my release date. The actual date was wrong, and I had to spend an extra two weeks at the facility. In my head, I was upset about the situation. The counselor explained to me that after my release, I would have to stay at my mother's house until the papers were approved. I was fine with staying at my mom's house. I felt like it gave me time to decompress before going to Columbus.

The boss gave me a recommendation to transfer to another Bob Evans in the Columbus area when I left. My dreams and aspirations for Columbus were focused on working in a recovery facility as peer support. I often thought about the true potential of this role. I knew that I would need to get certified. So, I began writing down my thoughts and ideas, and I created a list of facilities in the area in Columbus.

The day I left CBCF was an emotional one for me and my family. I remember going over to my grandmother's house. When I saw her for the first time, I cried with my head in her lap. She was so shocked to see me and so happy that I was healthy. The day I was arrested, I was six foot three inches tall and weighed 150 pounds. Now coming home, I was six feet three inches tall and 200 pounds. I was a completely different person. I told her I was so sorry for all the hurt I had caused the family. I told her things were going to be different this time around. I was so grateful that God had allowed me to see her again. It truly was answered prayers for me to be able to experience that moment.

That same day, I saw my sister for the first time since my arrest. I hugged her and started crying. I knew deep down that our relationship needed the most work. I had written to her over the years, and she expressed to my mom that she didn't want any of the letters. I couldn't blame her after all the years of fighting and the lying I did. It had created a massive void between us. The last time we had talked was around the same time I'd told her I would kill her. Naturally, she'd been living with that for years now. I knew this was going to take time; however, I didn't hesitate to ask if I could give her another hug. She was standoffish, but she came around to hug me back. I started crying again, telling her that I was sorry for all the pain I had put her through and for the pain our family had endured.

Both of our fathers were never there for us, and her father was extremely abusive growing up. My sister didn't remember her father, but I did. There was always this rift that she and I had. What I remembered of him was filled with pain. My mother had the worst of both worlds because she went through the abuse of both men. As a mother, she did what was best for us and left both men to protect us. My recovery is far from over. This is just a different chapter in the healing process, not only for me but for my family. I told my sister I would rather look back and know that I had tried than to grow old knowing that I'd never tried to make amends at all.

My coming home was nothing like what I had anticipated during my incarceration. Everything I thought I would say didn't come out. Everything I thought was going to play out didn't work out the way I had envisioned. I guessed this was just a glimpse into what it was going to be like for me, and I needed to be open-minded to that. Jordan told me his list of ideas had never come to fruition, and he was better off in life now than he had ever planned.

I remember him also telling me it's not always about what you know or who you know. Sometimes life works out in a way that is determined by being in the right place at the right time. There's opportunity everywhere in life; we just have to be open-minded to how the universe is going to present it to us. So here I am at the right place at the right time, and if one door closes, another one opens. This is my approach in life.

Journal entry, March 2016:

Today is a new day, and I am a free man. My whole life is in front of me with a fresh new start. Columbus, here I come.

6.

A New Way of Life

April 1, 2016, my first day in Columbus, Ohio. My aunt drove me to the Embark house, where I was greeted by my navigator, Tom, along with several other members of Embark. The navigator is the volunteer who is there upon your release to the Embark program. They help you with establishing basic scheduled routines, things like going to a meeting or the grocery store and even church. The times are coordinated between the individual and the navigator. This partnership lasts one year prior to your release and for the first year out, or until the Embark participant graduates the program—whichever comes first.

I toured the house and was shown to my room, where they had a laundry basket filled with towels, washcloths, and hygiene products. Everything was given to me through various church programs and volunteers. The house was furnished and stocked with food. This was such a humbling experience. Every one of us men and women in the program had an idea of the house and what to expect while we were still incarcerated. It's different when you finally come home and see it and experience it for the first time. It's no longer an idea or thought. The house is real. The kitchen, the yard, your privacy—it's all actually real.

It's overwhelming in a good way because you're experiencing it all in real time and everything seems to go so fast. No more count time, and no more hearing the sound of keys jingling from the corrections officers walking around. Your freedom and the world around you are moving at a pace that isn't considered when you're incarcerated.

My navigator asked me if I was hungry, and naturally I said yes. He and another navigator took me for a drive into downtown Columbus. They showed me around before going to a local restaurant called Hot Chicken Takeover.

The restaurant was in the North Market, where several other shops were located. Food vendors, coffee baristas, an ice cream shop, and also a butcher were just a few options offered within this marketplace. The North Market was a melting pot of restaurants and shops catering to the downtown Columbus area. Hot Chicken Takeover was unique in its approach to Southern fried hot chicken. It created a culture within its business model. Not only was the food amazing, but the creator's vision of bringing people together through his business model and food was genius. Hot Chicken Takeover's founder had partnered with Embark to give the men and women an opportunity for employment. The two missions aligned in a way that created a wonderful opportunity for both organizations.

As I was waiting in line to order my food, my navigator gave me a summary of the restaurant and how these two organizations came to work together. I remember looking at the menu and trying to figure out which level of spiciness I wanted. Next thing I knew, a lady came over and began adjusting the menu. Each day the restaurant started with a chicken count, which was written on the chalkboard. Once the chicken was gone, business was done for the day.

So, there I was standing in line when a beautiful woman came up with a clipboard in her hand. That's when I noticed the two bracelets on her wrist. One said, *I Am Second* and the other one said *Recovery is Beautiful*. This is where things got interesting because I had the exact same bracelets on my wrist. I thought, *There's no way this is a coincidence.* I politely said, "I'm sorry, I couldn't help but notice your bracelets. I have the same two." She turned around and with the most beautiful green eyes and perfect smile she looked at my wrist.

As I showed her my bracelets I asked, "So are you in recovery or is it someone you know?" She began to explain to me her clean time and then asked me how I got my *I Am Second* bracelet. I told her it was a ministry program I took while I was incarcerated. I explained to her that I had just gotten out of prison and that I was part of an organization called Embark. She kind of blushed and laughed and said she was too. I could feel my heart pounding in my chest, and I could feel my face and ears getting red. I thought to myself, *This is too much of a coincidence.* I didn't want to make it awkward, so I thought fast and asked what meal she recommended.

She told me that the warm boneless breast with mac and cheese and coleslaw was the best. I then asked her if she attended any of the Embark reunions. Every quarter or so, Embark had a get-together at one of several churches in Columbus where they were involved. Volunteers, members, and graduates got together to fellowship and spend time with one another. It was a great opportunity to network, and it built a community for those who might not have as much support from family and friends as others did. She said yes, she did attend reunions. I formally introduced myself to her by shaking her hand and telling her my name. The moment she touched my hand and told me her name, my whole life changed.

I thought to myself, *I just got home from prison. The last thing I should be focusing on is any kind of relationship.* The way we just met was something I couldn't help but question, though. As I was eating lunch, I couldn't help but think about the conversation I just had with Shannon. I wanted to know more about her but I needed to stay focused. It was hard because my first impression of her was how amazingly beautiful she was. I was definitely going to keep an eye out for Shannon at the next reunion.

My first night in the Embark house was strange because for the first time in almost five years I was alone. I rode my bike through the neighborhood and looked at all the beautiful houses in the area. The Embark house was located on the edge of a prominent section of Columbus called Bexley. This area was known for its historic and close-knit neighborhoods. Its highly ranked public school system and its status as the home of Capital University were prominent staples in the area. Call me crazy but I drew that energy in. It motivated me and I was inspired for more in life.

I loved how the houses looked, and I noticed how quiet the area was. The manicured landscaping was refreshing to see. Each mansion reminded me of a house you would find in a real estate magazine. I would go for runs in the morning and admire how nice and fresh everything seemed. The sprinkler systems would come on and the vehicles leaving for work were all high-end. I sensed structure and stability when I looked at these homes. I wondered about these homeowners' stories. Was it all from wealth, or did any of them come from middle-class or less-fortunate family dynamics? Were some of their life stories similar to mine?

I asked myself, *Where do I fit into all of this?* It was hard not to imagine if I had a chance to one day find myself in one of these neighborhood settings. Life is full of potential. Remember, it's not always what you know or who you know. Sometimes it's a matter of being at the right place at the right time. At that point, what are you going to do with that information? Sometimes you have to take a leap of faith and go all in.

I knew I had a long road to success ahead of me. Regardless, I wasn't going to let that deter me from where I wanted to be in life. Within my first two weeks of being home from prison, I landed my first job with a plastics manufacturer working the night shift. Embark's collaborations and partnerships with other organizations allowed me the resources to find employment through an organization called TAPP. The acronym stands for Training Assessment Placement Project. This is an organization designed with the purpose of providing second-chance employment to restored citizens and veterans. The program partnered with several other organizations in Ohio, including the Ohio Department of Rehabilitation and Corrections, Ohio Means Jobs, and Central Ohio Restored Citizens Collaborative (CORCC), just to name a few. The company that hired me was Engineered Profiles.

My first day trying to sleep after working the night shift is a memory I will never forget. Coming home from prison and finally having a real job with real responsibilities was an experience all on its own. It felt like it took forever for me to calm my mind before falling asleep. I was completely over-stimulated. Once I did fall asleep, though, it wasn't too long afterward that I woke up to the realization of how fast everything had taken hold in my life.

I had a rush of emotions overcome me: relief, gratitude, anxiety, exhaustion, and elation. The love and support that I had received along the way was more than I had ever expected. I figured things would have been more black and white in the sense of structure. What I was experiencing was acclimation back into society. The only thing I felt I could do was go downstairs and pray on my hands and knees, asking God for help. I told God I was scared and knew I couldn't do this alone. I asked Him to help guide me.

I opened my Bible, and as I was praying, my tears fell upon the book. As I wiped my tears off the pages, I realized I had opened to a section that had previously been highlighted from a prior study. In that moment I saw that it was Jeremiah 29:11-14, which says:

> *For I know the thoughts that I think toward you, saith the LORD, thoughts of peace, and not of evil, to give an expected end. Then shall ye call upon me, and ye shall go and pray unto me, and I will hearken unto you. And ye shall seek me, and find me, when ye shall search for me with all your heart. And I will be found of you, saith the LORD: and I will turn away your captivity, and I will gather you from all the nations, and from all the places whither I have driven you, saith the LORD, and I will bring you again into the place whence I caused you to be carried away captive.*

For me, God was telling me I wasn't alone. He heard me and He was there guiding me. He was telling me not to lose sight of His presence through the distractions and emotions of the world.

The confirmation that God heard me was not only marked by tears in that moment, they were highlighted.

I was reminded I wasn't alone in this journey anymore, even though it felt like I was. I took a deep breath, focused on my breathing, and began speaking out loud all the things I was grateful for. I named all the positive things I had going for myself. I made a gratitude list and wrote out all the plans and intentions I had for my future. It was at that moment that I recalled the first time I learned about the law of attraction. While in bed I began thinking of what my new life was going to feel like.

Everything is vibrational. God has blessed us with the ability to create. The more you stay in tune with those frequencies, the more likely they will align in your life. For me it's being aware that ultimately, it's God's timing. After all, we are heirs to his kingdom. Why wouldn't God want us to have abundance? Then I thought about how good it felt to get my first job.

It wasn't too long after I started working that Jordan came and visited me within my first month of being at the Embark house. He took me out for lunch and bought me dress clothes, running shoes, and groceries until I could start saving money. He also asked me if I was interested in doing a painting job. This was the same job he had done years ago when he first got out of prison. The job consisted of 250 mailboxes in an upscale neighborhood through an HOA. I took on the project and it cost me $500 for equipment and materials. When I finished the project I was paid $3,000. I painted on my days off, and in total it took me about a month to finish.

This side job was perfect for my schedule because I would spend my days off painting. The paint and the new numbers for the addresses were provided per the contract to the job bid. The contract also provided an ATV so I could get around, a generator, and the paint to use for my paint gun. I bought the paint gun and a shop vac to clean up all the paint chips as I scraped the old paint off each mailbox. This side job was perfectly set up. The money not only helped me financially but it also helped me build confidence in myself through trying something new. I saw the bigger picture behind how valuable my time could be when I utilized it strategically and the importance of time management.

When it came to my factory job I was starting to see how long it was taking me to get there using the bus. I quickly realized it was faster to ride my bike than to rely on Columbus' bus system. Using the bus took about two hours each way. This meant a total of four hours daily on the bus. I could ride my bike and be there in twenty-five minutes. Right before I started riding my bike to work, a random guy approached me at a bus stop. He asked me if I wanted to buy suboxone strips from him. (Suboxone is a medication used to prevent withdrawals from opioids, but it can also be abused to get high with and is highly addictive.)

I told him no; I was on parole. Then I said, "Let me ask you a question since you felt the need to offer me drugs. What are you doing, man? You're selling your suboxone, which tells me you're still addicted to opioids. Are you in a program right now?"

The guy replied, "Yes."

I told the guy, "You should reevaluate what you're doing. I've been clean for almost five years and just got out of prison because of drugs." Drugs had nearly ruined my life. I told him, "Ask yourself this question: How many people do you know that are dead that you used to get high with?" Then I told him, "Life doesn't have to be like this, man. You can get clean and you don't need the suboxone. You just need to be done and find a way to get clean cold turkey. Until that time comes, you're going to be stuck relying on what you are doing now. You're spreading poison."

He didn't want to hear that from me. He started walking away, and I was fine with that. At least I was able to speak some truth into his life, and I knew he needed to hear it.

I knew at that moment the devil had this man doing his bidding, and he couldn't even see it because he was desensitized by his drug use. I was grateful for God building me up and giving me the strength to stand up and say no to temptation. I was able to sit there at the bus stop that day and take a big breath of air, and it felt amazing. That's when it occurred to me that I could have already been at work had I ridden my bike.

As time progressed with life and work, I still thought about Shannon. Finally, my first Embark reunion since being home came, and Shannon was there. The same feelings from when I first met her came back up. I knew I was in trouble; there was something special about her. I just had to maintain my composure and not screw it up by chasing her off. I didn't want to come on too strong or for it to be bad timing. There were priorities in my life I was still working on, and I didn't want to be overzealous. Talking to her was nice, and I felt like I knew her a little better by the end of the event. I still didn't ask if she wanted to meet up sometime after work. It felt like it was too soon.

As I continued riding my bike to work, I used the time as motivation. I focused on the end goal of getting a vehicle and saving money for my first place. After a few months of working nights, I switched positions and got into the material handling department operating forklifts. Night shift was rough, especially trying to go to sleep during the day, so I had to make a decision. I knew working this job wasn't going to be forever, but for the time being I had to make it work. I pivoted and got on the day shift. The training I had in prison taught me how to drive a forklift, which allowed me this opportunity.

It was a relief switching shifts. Even though deep inside I felt trapped, I had insurance and I was saving money. The best part about my job was Mrs. Stacy. She oversaw the floor for the materials department. She had an open-door policy that made you feel like you mattered. Her ability to multitask and talk to anyone was a special gift that stood out to me. When I say "anyone," I mean anyone. From the CEO of the company to the degenerate who didn't last a week, she still made time to listen to you. She knew my situation and how I wanted more in life, and as much as she wanted me to stay, she also encouraged me to be better than the day before. I just couldn't shake the fact that my soul was telling me there was more in life for me. I really wanted to find my place as a recovery coach for peer support.

On my days off I called the ADAMH Board, which is the Ohio Department of Mental Health and Services Board, and left emails and voicemails looking for any kind of suggestive advice in order to get started. I also applied to half a dozen different job leads in Columbus. It was not easy, and in the end not a single facility called me back. I made several attempts for months on end trying to get a response. Each week I would call back hoping for someone to answer. By mid-July I was so busy with work and trying to finish the mailboxes that I had to make a decision. I had to put that dream on the back burner. At times I was working two weeks straight on twelve-hour shifts that I had to coordinate with the HOA about finishing the mailbox job.

My housing situation with Embark was good for at least a year, so my main focus was restitution and a car. When I was sentenced to prison I was also fined by the courts for my crimes. In total my fines were several grand. My main financial obligation upon release was paying those fines off as soon as possible. Any money left over I saved for a car. The way I figured out my restitution budget was by taking the total amount and dividing it by ten. I chose ten because I wanted to have the fines paid off in less than a year. Once I had that number I divided it by four. Now I had the weekly amount needed in order to make my payments. As for my vehicle I didn't even have one picked out yet. I just felt that $5,000 was a good starting point.

During the month of July I also celebrated my first birthday as a free man. My mom and two aunts came to Columbus and celebrated the day with me. They took me out for lunch, and it was nice to spend the day with them. While growing up, I had a close relationship with all my family. It wasn't until I got older that I began to feel a distancing from everyone, and it was because of my drug use. Out of all my family I was closest to my Uncle Doug while growing up.

In 1993 I spent the summer with him and his family in Ohio before we moved to Ohio permanently. Once that summer ended, I returned to Texas to start school again. In 1994 my mom decided to move to Ohio, and I stayed with my Uncle Doug once more. He was the closest thing I had to a father. He and his wife Jan had three daughters, whom I terrorized as a child. I was the annoying boy cousin who came up to visit and disrupted their summer. All they wanted to do was hang out and play with all their friends and girlfriends.

In 2002, tragically and unexpectedly, Doug and Jan's youngest daughter passed away in a car accident. She had just got her license, and a couple weeks later she was involved in the wreck. It was a hard time for the whole family. Even as time goes by the pain is still tender and hard to talk about. Since then their whole side of the family has grown. We as cousins are adults now, and we are close but in a different way.

Time doesn't stop when you go to prison. People get older. Families grow, and society continues. Some of my best childhood memories were while staying at Doug and Jan's. There was a sense of safety that came from staying at Doug and Jan's. They took me in as one of their own. I remember the first summer staying at their house. They would leave the windows open during the summer evenings, and the front door was always unlocked. It was a different time.

We didn't have to lock our bikes up or worry about an intruder. Everyone knew everyone. That was unorthodox to me at first. I came from Houston, Texas. It was rough and loud and busy. They lived in a small country town. Time slowed down when I lived with them. Doug was the one who taught me how to fish and who used to take me out hunting. I know I hurt him during my addiction. I reached out to him asking for help before prison. I didn't make it a week, and ultimately I turned around and went back to using.

A year later I ended up in prison. Naturally, our relationship had become strained. He never came to see me in prison for an official visit. He did, however, come to a few events that I was a part of while at Marion Correctional. He was also at my court hearings out of support for me, though I felt my mother needed the support more. I knew why he never visited. I understood how hard it must have been knowing there was nothing he could have done. I know it must have been tough watching me make the choices I made that sent me to prison.

But now things are different and we are closer than we have ever been. After coming home, I called him and told him I was living in Columbus. This is when our relationship began to grow. Since then we talk on a regular basis and get together regularly for a good cigar during family get-togethers, holidays, and family events.

I have another uncle, Uncle Greg. Greg is very professional and business-oriented. Most important, though, is his close relationship with Jesus Christ. Even though we weren't very close growing up, it wasn't anything personal. It was because he lived farther away. Surprisingly, he visited me quite often while I was in prison. He drove from Ann Arbor, Michigan, to visit me with my mom when I first got to Lorain. He also made a few surprise visits to Marion over the years. During my incarceration we would write to one another and share scripture. He even bought me a few books, which helped me pass the time in prison. Books like *Think and Grow Rich* by Napoleon Hill, *In It to Win It* by Steven J. Lawson, and *The Power of Focus* by Jack Canfield, just to name a couple. These books really helped me to open my mind, driving me even deeper into reading more literature. My family really did step up in their own unique ways, supporting me on my new path.

I've come to realize over the years that I'm worth more as an individual than just settling for complacency in life. I'm not going to allow my surrounding environment to determine my peace of mind. While in prison, I would often think to myself how I didn't want a nine-to-five to determine my outcome in life. I wanted to build something more for myself that I could look back on and say was mine. I wanted to be independent. I wanted to leave a legacy behind. I'm still working on what that legacy looks like, but writing *Emersion* was the start to making my vision come to fruition.

Ninety days after my release, I was scheduled to return home for a ninety-day review with the judge. My navigator volunteered to drive me. At the time, I was working twelve-hour shifts and riding my bike five miles one way. My shift was six pm to six am. That morning, after work, I changed into my dress clothes in the bathroom and got into Tom's car to head to court. It was nice to spend the day with him and reflect on how life had been since coming home. My navigator would often pick me up and take me to church when I first came home. He even invited me to his church to bake cookies for one of the upcoming Kairos events. The same cookies that were given to me while I was in prison, I was now helping bake. I remember praying over the cookies, asking that God reach every individual who was to receive the cookies, that they would hear God's voice and receive His Holy Spirit. It was truly a remarkable experience.

When we got to court, my mom and Uncle Greg were there, and they were officially able to meet my navigator. Once the court started the judge pulled out a folder and asked me to talk about the programs I had completed. As I covered everything, I also explained to him that early on in my incarceration, I committed to changing my life. I was determined to do whatever was necessary to achieve that goal. I began to explain how I had wanted to get clean before I got arrested, and I told him that prison saved my life.

As I continued to speak about each program, the judge started going through the folder of certificates I had sent in for review. I could see the smile on his face as he sorted through the documents. He then stopped to look at me and stated, "In all my years as a judge, I have never experienced an individual that I sent to prison transform their lives in such a manner as you have."

I said, "Yes, sir." I told the judge that four and a half years ago I couldn't stay in this courtroom for more than thirty minutes without wanting to leave because I was ashamed. The guilt was so heavy at the time that it pained me to make eye contact. Today I could stand there and talk for hours about my life and the experiences I had getting to know God. I explained to the judge that I wished there could have been a better way than to go to prison. However, the outcome wouldn't have been the same.

The judge and I talked about God for at least forty-five minutes, and he even explained to me why he was so firm on drug charges. He began to explain how he had seen the heroin epidemic destroy his community. In all my life I had never had a good experience in court until that day. I was glad it was going to be my last time having to stand before him in this courtroom. I was truly a changed man, and for once in my life I didn't have to explain myself like I once did. My actions did that for me now. Vindication was an understatement as I left the courthouse that day. Everyone, including the judge, told me how proud they were of me. This is what change looks like. This is what hard work paying off feels like. All those years of journaling and all the programs I took to change my life were all falling into place now.

After court we all went out to eat. Afterward we drove back to my hometown. We drove past the high school I had graduated from. I showed my navigator the house I grew up in and the bike trails I used to ride on as a kid. It was a very special experience being able to share that with him. During our time driving through town, memories of my childhood came back to me. Times of running around after school as a kid and even times when I was older and in high school. Everything had changed. The elementary school I went to had been torn down, and the high school had been turned into a middle school/high school campus. None of it was the same, and it was impressive how much had changed in the few years I was in prison. It was also confirmation that this wasn't my home anymore.

How I wish I could go back and do things differently, I thought. On our drive back to Columbus, we talked about how it felt visiting the town I had grown up in again. I told him it didn't even feel like home anymore, and I knew that it was time to move on. It was a bittersweet moment as we drove out of town. I realized I was focusing on what was in front of me rather than what was behind me.

That same week my Uncle Greg called to tell me that he got the family to put money together and help find me a vehicle. I just had to pay for the taxes and the tags. I had just recently gotten my driver's license so it couldn't have come at a better time. The day I got my vehicle was one I will never forget. The feelings were stimulating as I drove down the same streets I rode my bike on to get to work. Every day as I rode my bike to work, I would imagine what it would feel like driving again. Living the feeling as it played out was way better than I could have ever imagined.

I was humbled by the perspective, and I couldn't help but think about how much God had blessed me. It's amazing just how powerful our minds are when it comes to tapping into the possibilities of creating our future. God is limitless. The rainy days before and after work that I had to endure while riding that bike from point A to point B were prime examples of determination. It feels good achieving the goals you set for yourself. Those experiences only drove my motivation that much more. Deep inside I knew people were trusting in me. During those times of adversity, I felt that the devil was testing me, wanting me to quit. I believe the devil loves failure and wants nothing more than for people to be miserable. To me, it was known all too well as self-sabotage. I know God's true intentions for my life now. It's because of that that the joy of success supersedes all the negativity.

August came around, and Shannon and I decided to meet in German Village at Schiller Park. My sixth anniversary of living in Columbus after being released from prison was right around the corner. We met in the park and ate pizza. I was so nervous but excited about spending time with her. It felt like being a kid again. Everything about her made me feel rejuvenated. I was excited to see her, and she made me feel happy. I was intrigued to learn more about her and hear more of her story. Having so much in common truly amazed me, especially when I would think back to how we had first met.

It was compelling listening to her share her experiences with addiction and the struggles she had growing up. There was a passion that came from her that I was all too familiar with. More importantly I was captivated by how she had come to know God and how God was working in her life. We talked about goals and intentions for our individual lives. It came to a point where we decided to go for a walk around the park, and for the first time we held hands. I'll never forget this day, because I truly believe God prepared us both for that moment together.

I remember sitting on a bench in the park with her, and she asked me what I thought about meeting for the first time. I paused for a moment. I knew what I wanted to say. I had never felt stronger about meeting someone before in my life. In that moment I remember closing my eyes for a split second, and I asked God for the words. I heard God speak to me and say, "If you lead, she will follow." I told her what God wanted me to say. I also said I wanted to honor God and continue to build our relationship with Him in it.

I told Shannon I believed God had prepared us for that moment, and I wanted to continue talking and getting to know her. I wanted us to share our relationship with God. She looked away for a second, and as she looked back at me she had a huge smile on her face. She said, "I've been praying for God to prepare me for this moment in my life as well. I agree that God allowed us to meet." On August 21, 2016, Shannon and I started dating. It's silly, because there I was, thirty-five years old, and it felt like my first girlfriend all over again. I know it may sound immature, but ever since I had met Shannon I couldn't stop thinking about her.

I thought I was losing my mind, but I continued to pray about things and ask God for guidance. An event would come up and I would see her there. A concert at a church would come around, and she would be there. All the small details, like our bracelets and the people we knew. God was behind all that, so why question it? Without a doubt in my mind, I knew Shannon and I meeting was God's intentional and divine power at work.

Think about this: Out of all the places and all the people in the world. Out of all the people Shannon had seen and met prior to me being released from prison and coming to Columbus. How is it that years after her release I came home and we met the same day I moved to Columbus? Only to find each other in the manner that we did. The probability is so far out there that in my eyes it was all God's doing. Deep down I knew I was going to marry this woman someday. I didn't tell her that right away, though.

September rolled around, and I was anxiously approaching five years clean. On September 23 I was excited and more motivated than ever before. I had often journaled while incarcerated about hitting the five-year mark. To me this was a major milestone and one to be proud of. A personal accomplishment that I had looked forward to ever since I had achieved one year clean. Not only is September 23 my clean date, but it was also my friend Big Country's birthday.

I called him and wished him a happy birthday and shared with him that I was five years clean. I didn't do it to rub it in his face. I did it because I knew he was proud of me for overcoming such a horrible addiction, one that most people can't find their way out of.

I knew early on I couldn't move back home. The town wasn't big enough for me, and I needed more opportunities. The economy back home just couldn't offer what I was in search of. My hometown was plagued by constant reminders of my past, and I needed to move on from that. I spent my day celebrating it with Shannon. We went out to eat and then to a Narcotics Anonymous meeting.

We were joined by a few other friends of ours that evening. I was presented with my five-year coin in celebration of my personal accomplishment with recovery. It was a great way to end the day and start a new year of continuing in my recovery. With everything going on in my life, things just continued to progress. I expressed to Shannon that I truly cared deeply about her and opened up a little more to her about my true feelings. I trusted her enough now that I told her about my idea behind writing a book, and I shared some of my writings. I told her that I believed my poem "When I Imagine" was me manifesting her into my life.

September was an amazing month for me, and what better way to close it out than to go skydiving? Paul, who had been in prison with me, also happened to be a graduate of the Embark program. He lived at the house at the same time as I did. He invited me to go skydiving. I was a little hesitant at first, but the more he talked about it, the more I was open to taking the jump. To me five years of clean time and being released from prison was a great reason to take a "leap of faith" in this new chapter in life, so I did.

When I Imagine

As I lay here with my hands on my chest staring at the ceiling,
I find myself thinking about that special someone.
I imagine if I ever meet her, what will she look like?
I imagine what makes her laugh, what her favorite foods are,
and what her favorite music is.

I imagine staring into her eyes as if they were
from a kaleidoscope.
I imagine running my fingers through her hair,
as if it was that of silk.
The concept of time is nonexistent
and the worries of the world are lost.
I never imagined this void to be so intense, or that these
emotions would become my prison in this pursuit of her.
I imagine the world to be so much smaller
than what it truly appears to be,
Only When I Imagine!

Skydiving was the most daring thing I have ever done besides using heroin. The plane flight to our jump height was insane. It was a small plane that seated no more than twelve people. The whole time I just kept thinking, *I can't believe I'm actually doing this.* You could feel every bit of turbulence. The only thing separating me from the outside was a sliding door and a seatbelt. Once my time to jump came, we were at 12,000 feet, and I could see the curvature of the Earth's atmosphere. Words do not give the experience justice.

So much was happening in my life, and it seemed to be happening all at once. I got a job, I acquired my license, I got my first vehicle. I just hit five years clean, I was in a new relationship, and now I was going skydiving. I know it may all sound simple, but as I was living it, life was going by fast. As everything was happening in my life, I was asked by one of the Embark members how I felt about starting to look for my first place. I was kind of caught off guard by the question at first. I wasn't expecting to move for at least another six months.

He went on to tell me that "out of everyone in the house we feel you're the most prepared, and so we thought we would ask." I told him I needed to run it by my parole officer. As long as she was okay with it, then I was fine with it. It took me a few days before my parole officer got back to me to say it was okay. I told Shannon about it, and she said she would talk to her landlord and see if he had any places available. It was because of her that I ended up finding my first place. Her landlord had a spot on the West Side of Columbus about ten minutes from where she lived. The house was nice even though it wasn't in the best area of Columbus.

I decided to take the place because I knew it was temporary. At thirty-five years old, I was able to financially depend on myself. October rolled around, and I moved into my first apartment. Utilities were in my name, and for the first time in my adult life I had my very own place. Embark helped me with a furniture bank voucher. It was there I got a refrigerator, washer, dryer, stove, and a bed with lamps and a couple end tables. My place had the basic furniture, and it was a good start. I had what was needed to survive, and that's all that mattered.

The furniture voucher Embark helped provide was nothing short of a miracle. I couldn't believe how every major appliance that I needed happened to be there at the same time. The volunteer who took me even told me that he'd never seen anyone walk away with all those things in one visit. I remembered telling the volunteer that there are no coincidences with God. To this day I still have the dryer and the refrigerator. I remember calling Shannon and telling her about how I'd made out, and even she was impressed by it. I couldn't help but laugh. Even though I had my own place now, I was mainly staying at Shannon's place with her.

Every day after work I would go to my place to check on things, and from time to time we would stay at my place. Eventually my place got the rest of the furniture needed to feel like home. I bought a kitchen table with chairs and a couch and a TV stand. On Wednesday, October 12, 2016, after I got cleaned up from work, we went out shopping. I remember getting the worst headache out of nowhere.

It was so bad that we had to leave the store. Shannon took me to get something to eat because I hadn't eaten yet. We grabbed Arby's because it was nearby. My headache was still bad, and I couldn't figure out why I had this migraine; I never got headaches. I remember going back to her place to eat, and that's when I got the phone call that changed my life forever. My dear friend Big Country had passed away from a drug overdose. I dropped to the floor and just cried. During my headache I knew something wasn't right. Now it made perfect sense. My friend of twenty-two years was gone.

I believe my spirit was telling me something was wrong. It was why I got that headache. I truly believe without a doubt that there's no coincidence I got that headache and then got the phone call that he was dead. I thought back on our past. We were just kids doing kids' stuff. He was like a brother to me, and that day I lost him. Everything stopped at that moment. The pressure in my head went away, but now there was this emptiness in the pit of my stomach. I lost my appetite, and Shannon just held me as I cried in her lap. I finally came to terms with the fact that he was gone about a half hour later. At that moment nothing else mattered. All I could think about was going home for his funeral.

I called his parents the next day and found out that the funeral was set for a Monday. I told them I wanted to be a pallbearer. I drove home that weekend and attended the funeral. I got there before anyone else did. I wanted to spend time with him before the service started. It didn't even look like him. I held his hand as he lay in his casket, and I just started bawling. I got on my knees and prayed to God and just held his hand and envisioned Big Country happy and at peace now.

It hurt so much knowing his time had come. It almost looked as if he had been crying, because it was kind of wet in the corner of his eye. I just told him I was sorry again and told him I loved him. Slowly people started trickling in for the funeral. I talked with everyone I knew, trying to understand what had happened. Apparently he had been at a drug house helping someone move. After they left he stayed there, got high, and passed away in the basement. They didn't come back for a couple of days, when they found Big Country. There were a lot of old friends from back in high school and a lot of his family I hadn't seen since before prison. People were surprised to see me.

Some thought I was still in prison, while others were shocked to see how much I had grown and changed. It felt awkward because we were no longer kids. We were grown up now, and most of them had families of their own. As I wrestled with these realizations, flashback memories of the people I saw reminded me of simpler times. Subconsciously, I still felt a piece of my childhood inside me, reminding me of the years when I lacked self-confidence. For some reason, seeing everyone brought up old insecurities within myself that I used to carry when I was younger. I was able to shake it off and realized that that was the old me.

The more I thought about Big Country's passing, the more it pained me to know that he had never beaten his addiction. I just kept praying for his soul. I know he believed in Jesus because we used to talk about him from time to time. I knew he was saved; however, I felt it was necessary to clear the air with him for his journey to heaven.

During the funeral I spoke and encouraged the room to remember his qualities, not his imperfections. He loved being outside. He loved fishing and riding dirt bikes and four-wheelers. He loved children and enjoyed listening to country music. He liked his coffee in the morning and whisky in the evening. He could be your best friend or your worst enemy, but he was always able to make you laugh. The pastor spoke that day, and I was reminded of the scripture from Proverb 3:5-6:

> Trust in the Lord with all thine heart;
> And lean not unto thine own understanding.
> In all thy ways acknowledge him,
> And he shall direct thy paths.

I spoke on this scripture because I believed that it wasn't for us to understand right now why God had decided to allow his passing. I think it is more important to know that he is in a better place now, rather than to hold onto the suffering we knew he had. It was hard being there, because his parents and brother were still getting high at the time. His mom and dad sat up front, nodding off in an obvious escape from personal anguish and pain. The family had never been the same since Cody's passing. Now they were dealing with the loss of another son. The loss of two sons in fifteen years is an absolute tragedy. Words cannot describe how disturbingly sad it was to watch this family crumble from pain, anguish, and emotional turmoil over the years.

After the funeral I sat by Big Country's grave and talked with his youngest brother, Ryan. I told him that his drug use had to stop. "You're going to fucking die. Please just stop!" All he could say was that he knew and he was going to change. I gave him a hug and just started crying again. It was painful to accept the loss of Big Country and to think about the pain his whole family had endured. It was humbling to know how hard I'd worked to get clean. I also knew deep down inside that it was possible for anyone to change.

I just wish that everyone had the same passion as I did to want a better life. We are blinded by an unseen matrix that allows us to be comfortable in our current situations. Creating a complacent approach to life leaves you blinded, and before you know it life passes you by. The same goes with addiction. I think about the people on the streets panhandling for drug money. I think of those I may know who are still in and out of jail because of their addictions. I just wish they all could wake up and experience reality like I did when my body was purged of heroin and drugs.

Big Country's passing was a prime example of what happens when we don't wake up. It's okay to question ourselves and embrace emotions we are uncomfortable with when it comes to change. Accept that sometimes growth equals pain. I didn't hold that back from Ryan. I let him hear it from the bottom of my heart, because I believed that no one else was going to say the things he needed to hear.

Big Country's passing was nothing short of devastation for not only his family but the whole community that knew him. To this day, I'm at a loss for words when reminded that he is gone. The grieving process is a real thing, and I don't even know what stage I'm in. Sometimes I'm doing fine, and then other days the realization hits me that he's gone. I can't help but stop and think about all the good times we had as kids and teenagers growing up. I thought to myself, *This town will never be the same.* The bike trails and streets that we once rode on would always hold childhood memories. Yet the trains that pass through and blow their horns are a haunting reminder of the pain from the past. The quietness in this town is a stark reminder of the emptiness that's been created from the loss of loved ones.

As much as I wanted to stay and visit longer, I knew I had to leave. My drive home felt empty. A part of my past was left behind that day. I thought I had done all the growing up that was needed to prepare me for this new life after incarceration. Big Country passing changed me in a way that made me feel even older now. I was looking forward to Big Country meeting Shannon. I was hopeful for experiencing things in life with him around. The knowledge of this not being possible now was heart-wrenching.

It had been only a month since I'd called and wished him a happy birthday. I remember telling him about Shannon and how excited I was for him to meet her. There were so many great things that were happening in life since coming home from prison. I wanted to share all of it with him. At the time I knew he was struggling, but I believed everything would be okay. It was hard to accept that he was gone. It pained me to know how bad off his mother, father, and youngest brother Ryan still were. It's a freaking nightmare, and there is nothing I can do but love them all from a distance.

From Your Eyes, I Know!

I've seen you for the first time in over four years
and in that moment "I know!"
You smile and it seems uncomfortable; your energy says
you're hiding something. You look down
in between eye contact and "I know."
Pinpoint pupils glazed over like glass and "I know."
You smile but your face tells a different story, your energy is
uneasy, I can feel your turmoil from a distance, "I know."
I hug you and I don't want to let go. It's been far too long,
my brother! Your eyes tell a story of struggle, your face is pale,
and you look tired. I feel like your soul
is screaming for help, "I know!"
I hug you and I don't let go, I tell you that I love you, I tell
you that I know. I tell you I'm sorry because I know your pain
all too well, I know your struggle, I know your confusion,
and I know how lost you are.
If I could take it all away I would; however,
this is your battle and it's something you have to do for
yourself, but you're not alone!
From your eyes I cry. From your eyes I cry because I'm
sorry for the void that has consumed your life.

> From your eyes I see desperation, screaming for a solution,
> screaming silently from within.
> From your eyes I know…
> All I want is for you to get well, for you to be happy again.
> For you to be clean.
> From your eyes to mine, I'm stricken with the knowledge
> of your pain, "I KNOW!"

November rolled around and Shannon and I started talking about the holidays and making plans. We both decided to do Thanksgiving together. I invited my family down, but everyone already had plans, so they weren't able to attend. Shannon's family came to Columbus, and it was nice to meet her grandparents for the first time. I had already met her mom and dad, so it was nice to spend time with them again as well.

We had ham, mashed potatoes and gravy, cornbread, scalloped potatoes, and green beans. Shannon's mom made deviled eggs, and I made a pumpkin roll for dessert. During dinner I sat at the table and reflected on everything. I couldn't help but think about how long it had been since I enjoyed a family holiday without drugs. Not to mention free and happy. I started to think about how Big Country's family was doing with him gone now. I wondered how they were holding up. I called the house and left a message because no one had answered.

Since Cody passed away in 2001, Big Country's family stopped celebrating the holidays. That's when I thought about something Shannon had shared with me when we first started dating. Her mom was still in active addiction, and Shannon wanted to get her mom help. I was all for it and told her I would do what I could. During dinner Shannon's mom seemed to be doing okay, but she didn't stay long once we were finished eating. Before she took off I drove her to the gas station to get some cigarettes, and we were able to talk on a more personal level.

She told me how nice it was to see her daughter happy, and that made me feel good. I knew that she was referring to our relationship. Thinking of her mom reminded me of when I was using. On the surface I was good at making things seem fine. Inside, my soul was hurting because I wanted to quit. I just didn't have the power to do it by myself back then. For me I needed to be locked up. I felt bad for both Shannon and Ryan. I couldn't imagine my mother being addicted to drugs. I've experienced firsthand for years the toxicity that is created when using drugs, but I couldn't relate to using with my mother or father.

Shannon and I spent Christmas apart. But even during those few days, I wanted to be back in Columbus close to her. I remember the first time I told her I loved her. It was definitely a memory I will never forget. For once in my life I could say I was in love and meant what I was saying. Telling Shannon I loved her was the first time doing so without any drugs in my system. To me our relationship was different from any relationship I'd been in before. For New Year's Eve, we spent it inside watching movies and talking about goals for the new year.

One thing that Shannon was excited about and planning for was her son coming to visit for the summer. I was happy for her, because when she went to prison her husband at the time just packed up and moved. He took her son from Ohio to Wyoming to start over. Shannon went through a lot of emotional healing during her years of incarceration. She had to get over her addiction and the feelings of abandonment associated with her child's father taking off on her. By springtime Shannon moved out of her apartment and into my place, and her mom finally moved to Columbus.

Her mother was able to get into a shelter, where she stayed until she could get into an all-women's recovery facility called Amethyst. Shannon knew of this place because of the all-women's AA group that she attended regularly. After a few months her mom was able to get housing through the Amethyst program. She was able to live there and utilize the therapy classes, focusing on her past and present drug usage. These programs allowed her mom the time she needed to emotionally heal and find a new way of living life without the use of drugs.

Shortly after Shannon's mom got into the Amethyst program, I proposed to Shannon. On May 25, 2017, I asked Shannon to marry me. I proposed during dinner at our place. Now, typically I would have made a big deal out of proposing, but Shannon was very private. I chose to do it while her mother was there. Shannon didn't even expect it, but I told her, "I've never been more certain about marrying anyone."

I told her we would figure life out together. I just couldn't have her walking around without a ring on her hand. That summer her son Dalton came to Ohio. We did everything in our power to make him feel welcome and comfortable. We went to the zoo and Kings Island at Six Flags to ride roller coasters. We went to the water park and watched fireworks on the Fourth of July. We did a lot of cooking out on the grill and even went hiking and kayaking. That summer was wonderful for us.

It was a prime example of how good life can be after prison and without drugs. Shannon and I are proof that there is a better way of life outside of addiction. You don't have to be defined by your past. You have to adopt the mindset that abundance is limitless in life. You just have to work really hard at harnessing the mental conviction that God is the abundance. He gives you the ability to literally create your deepest desires.

Even Shannon's mom realized she was able to find the strength within herself to get clean and heal. After years of recovery she is now in a place she can call her own. It takes hard work and dedication to overcome active addiction. The secret is to find that desire deep within yourself and imagine without a doubt what that life looks like. Early on for me it was a vision of happiness and a life free from incarceration and from drugs. A happy family and nice things that I never had while using.

It was a life that meant no restrictions. It meant freedom to travel and explore what the world had to offer. I accepted early on that there were going to be challenges and setbacks along the way. I knew that I wasn't going to take no for an answer, though. I was determined to find my place in life. My first job was a solid stepping stone, as it prepared me for new opportunities. It gave me a foot in the door with employment and time to manage my money. Did I like what I was doing? No! I was working twelve hours a day and it was hot and it was hard work.

It didn't stop me from striving for more and looking for better opportunities and possibilities. After prison one year turned into two, and before I knew it I had built my credit up and slowly began saving more money. At first it wasn't much. I was making thirteen dollars an hour and only saving a little over $100 a month, but I made it work. It wasn't easy and it took years of sacrifice, living paycheck to paycheck. What other choice did I have? I took the first thing that came my way. I wasn't going back to prison, and I needed money.

By late 2017 with all my fines paid off, money started to add up in my bank account. I was patiently waiting for a potential early release from parole/probation. Now my biggest challenge in life was finding a better-paying job/career. I prayed on it daily while thinking outside the box for job potentials. I often reflected on what life would look like and feel like making more money. To have more time to spend doing what I enjoyed, such as hiking, fishing, and spending time with family. In September I received a phone call of another dear friend passing away.

My friend Kyle, the guy I had written music with in prison, had died, apparently in a house fire. According to the newspaper article, they found him by the window in the upstairs apartment. The report said that the batteries in the smoke detectors had been removed and that he'd died from smoke inhalation. I was heavy with sorrow over the news of his death. I found myself again reflecting on the loss of another person I'd shared fond memories with.

Kyle had the ability to do anything he wanted with his music. He had his whole life ahead of him. His gift to play guitar and sing was amazing, and those songs we made and the music he played will always be remembered. Kyle introduced me to artists I never knew about, and thanks to him when I hear them I think of him. The most unfortunate situation about Kyle's unexpected death was that he had just recently come home from prison. He hadn't even been home a whole year yet. He was just getting back on his feet. It was another reminder of how precious our time on earth really is.

In 2018 a new job opportunity came around. I heard about a position at a glue factory called Franklin International. Franklin International was known for the popular wood glue Titebond. They make more than just that, but it was an interesting conversation piece when people would ask what I did for a living. When I learned that I got the job, I didn't hesitate to make the switch. The job came with a significant pay increase, and within six months after starting my new job I was able to get a new vehicle. In fact, this vehicle was the nicest one I had ever owned.

Until this point in my life, the best vehicle I'd ever had was worth $3,000, and now I was driving a brand-new vehicle. If you believe all you're ever going to have in life is the bare minimum, then you're limiting your potential. I'm reminded of the story of Jim Carey, the actor. He wrote a $10 million check to himself and kept it in his wallet. He believed there was more for himself and had a vision as to what that life looked like. He worked hard and continued to pursue his passion and dreams. The check he wrote was for services rendered from acting.

Do you know that that check came to fruition? Don't believe it? It's true. Look into it; it's quite an interesting story. There is plenty of supporting information on the internet in regards to the power of manifestation. I first learned about the Law of Attraction while I was in prison. The more I dug into understanding it, the more I began to realize how powerful God has made us. The year 2018 was amazing for Shannon and me, and it started out with us moving to a better part of Columbus.

This is the time we started talking about setting a wedding date. I had a new job and a new vehicle, and we got a new place together that year. The most intriguing part about 2018 was connecting with a long-lost sister of mine. That summer for my birthday, Shannon bought me a DNA test from 23andMe. I wanted to try and track down relatives on my father's side of the family. When my father passed away it devastated me. I didn't know anyone from my father's side. I hadn't seen my father since I was three, but I always had hope that someday I would meet him again.

Being told that he'd passed away crushed any dreams I ever had of meeting him again. The best memory I had of my father was when I was having a picnic with my mom and father. During that picnic everyone was happy. I remember playing with a little wooden wind-up airplane in a field with him. That's the only good memory I had of my parents together. When my mother broke the news of my father passing away, I believe that's when the last bit of my innocence was lost.

I felt the whole world around me get smaller. I remember asking questions about my relatives on my father's side. This is how I found out my father was from California. Most of my father's side of the family was gone, according to my mom. She just didn't have any more information for me as a kid. At twelve years old I had already been through a lot. The abuse from my stepfather was more than any child should ever have to experience.

Include the diagnosis of ADHD at the age of seven with a prescription for Ritalin three times a day, and it was just a lot for me personally. One thing I never lost sight of, though, was when my mom mentioned I had an older sister. I held onto that growing up, often wondering where she was and what her life was like. Now that I was clean and living a productive life, I wanted to know more about my family. Once the results came back, I started doing more research. 23andMe provided a database of information, but I didn't have any luck with being able to contact anyone. I began looking into my father's social security number and his death date on Ancestry.com. I cross-searched all his personal information with the State of California and the State of Hawaii, which is where my mother said my sister lived.

What I found was the name of a woman from California. After about two weeks of searching I was notified through Ancestry.com that a lady named Carrie had searched my father's name along with his social security number and death date a while back. I checked for a social media account and found one that matched the name and location. I talked to my wife about it, and she told me we should reach out, so I did. What happened next was mind-blowing. Turns out that Carrie was one of two older sisters.... Yeah, that's right, I had more than one sister.

My father had children with two other women prior to meeting my mom, and both sisters lived in California. At first I was apprehensive, because I thought about a potential scam or something. Once we started talking, I knew that this was real. Carrie went on to tell me about my other sister, Erica. I asked my mom, and she verified my sister's name was in fact Erica, but she didn't know about anyone named Carrie. Both Erica and Carrie had pictures of my father when he was younger. Carrie had my father's wallet, which I now have, and Erica had pictures of me as a little baby. Erica was the most informative about our father. She was the closest to my dad, grandpa, and grandma. She was there when my father passed away, and I missed my grandma's passing by a year.

Erica told me stories of how she used to write to my mom as a little girl asking about me, "her little baby brother." Finding each other forty years later was a very emotional time for all of us. For a good portion of my life, I knew I had a sister and just didn't know how to find her. Erica, on the other hand, was in contact with me only to lose it when my mom began moving around. We were both affected by this, though her experience was more real, because as a child she was writing to me.

It's sad to think about yet amazing that we found each other so many years later. My father was not a healthy person; he had both an addictive personality and mental health issues. I learned details related to these issues through my mother and by talking to Erica and Carrie. Their mothers left my father for the same reasons. He was tormented by his traumatic upbringing, which led to his issues of substance abuse. Being in a relationship with my father was clearly difficult for these women because he didn't know how to manage his emotions.

With all this new information and finding new family members I had never met before, it was overwhelming. I have since found family in California, Tennessee, Alabama, Missouri, and Mississippi. All on my father's side. Shannon and I began talking about going to California to meet Erica and Carrie, but the planning part was going to be challenging to figure out. Shannon and I were in the process of wedding planning, and life was busier than ever before. My new job was still very demanding, and even though the money was good I was still reeling with a deeper need for purpose in life.

I was still searching for clarity on what that purpose in life was, and at the time I was still only writing in my journal. By now it had been two years since Big Country's funeral. As often as I would drive back home to visit my mom, I would visit him and his brother's headstone. The thought that he was gone was hard, and I was still grieving over it. At first I would find myself at times feeling sadness while journaling and during meditation. I know he's looking down on me, and I know he's free from pain, yet the burden was still there.

Shortly after Big Country's passing, I had a dream about him. He was in an all-white T-shirt with white shorts and a white bandana. I was so sad in my dream because I missed him, and I remember hugging him. I was crying in my dream, and I told him I missed him. He looked at me and said, "Why are you crying? Don't be sad." And then he said, "I'm okay." His presence is felt the strongest when I least expect it.

Whether it's a song or while I'm fishing or working, I find myself reminded of him. It could be something we did together or something he did or said that I think of. That's when I know he is near. His passing has been the hardest to deal with since getting clean from heroin. When I'm reminded of him, I turn to God and ask Him for clarity. I'm constantly reminded of the scripture I touched on at his funeral, Proverbs 3:5. I believe without a doubt that God speaks to us through the universe. We just have to be open-minded enough to receive what it is that is being revealed.

It's like me writing this book. I took action with what I felt I was called to do. When I learned about the power of my thoughts, I knew God was showing me a deeper sense of my true potential. I look back on life now, and I'm able to create a timeline of events that have proven to me just how powerful this progression has been. I'm more in tune with myself now than ever. Once I was able to open my mind to the limitless possibilities for myself, I began to unfold all the layers of distraction.

Shannon bought me a laptop to begin writing my book. At the time I was doing a lot of soul searching, and this laptop couldn't have come at a better time for me. You can't worry about the what-ifs in life. If you worry about those distractions, you're never going to get anything done. At that moment in my life I knew I was supposed to write even more than before. I began by creating an outline of how I wanted my book structured. I pulled out all my old writings and began to piece them together. I began transferring them to the computer. The year 2019 was approaching, and my outlook was the same since I first got clean, optimistic, and driven. Out with the old in with the new.

In 2019 Shannon and I attended a concert by a Christian group called Bethel. We had been listening to them since we first started dating. We were excited to finally see them. During that event our experience was nothing short of amazing. It was so powerful; you could feel the Holy Spirit in the venue. I was so overwhelmed with a feeling of peace and gratitude during the show that I began to cry because of how humbled I was for my new life. I looked over, and Shannon was crying as well.

We just started to hug one another. Next thing I knew a couple beside us laid their hands on our shoulders and prayed over our lives. It was truly a blessing. I've never experienced that kind of unconditional love from complete strangers in public before. I knew God was there, and it was beautiful. The experience was profound for me, and that feeling of love was something I'm still reminded of to this day.

Through 2019 as I continued going to meetings, another friend of mine, Mark, came home from prison. Mark was the guy I said reminded me of Adam Levine from the band Maroon 5. I met Mark at a couple meetings when he first got out. I told him early on to let me know when he was ready to start working the steps, and I would help if he needed it. I helped him get the literature and workbook needed to get him on the right path. Yet after a couple of times of going to meetings with him, I didn't see or hear from him again for several months. Here is the truth that I learned in recovery that most people don't realize: You can't work another person's recovery for them, no matter how hard you try to help them.

As for someone who is active in recovery, you can only lead by example. One thing I gained from my incarceration was a purpose for my life. My purpose isn't unique to just me. It's a purpose that we all can adopt in life, which is to be a vessel of hope for others. There's so much in life that God is trying to show us, teach us, and prepare us for. If we continue to focus on failures, we are never going to be able to fully experience the abundance that God is trying to bless us with. The what-ifs are only going to limit you.

After three years of being with Shannon, we got married in July 2019. Not for one second was I concerned or afraid that I was making the wrong decision by marrying her. I've never been more certain in my entire life that I was meant to spend my life with her. She understands me more than I can understand myself at times, and it's amazing. I'm not surprised because we are both Cancers, which we joke about from time to time. During my addiction with heroin, I never thought I was going to have someone like her in my life, only because my outlook was more simplistic and narrow-minded back then. I just wanted to be clean from heroin.

We have encouraged one another and lifted each other up many times over the course of our covenant with one another. Even though it seems like a short time, a lot has happened to us and for us. A healthy relationship isn't simple; it takes work and commitment. We have had our differences in opinion and we have had our disagreements. I'm not going to pretend like we haven't. We both have similar backgrounds when it comes to our past lives of heroin addiction and incarceration. We have our traumas we are figuring out through healing. Our healing processes are unique to ourselves.

I can't do her work, and she can't do mine for me. Together, though, we are able to find closure during our times of difficulties, by sharing with one another our journey through therapy. The twelve steps have been amazing for me; however, there was something more that was missing. Doing research, reading, listening to podcasts, and journaling about my challenges have proven to be very beneficial over the years. Through recovery I was able to admit that I had a lot of resentments and anger issues from my past. It's because of that that I've worked on identifying and resolving my triggers based around those personal experiences of powerlessness. I've come to find that my responses stem from my childhood traumas.

My feelings of limitation stemmed from recurring reminders as a child of not having a father. The verbal and physical abuse from my stepfather were where the issues with powerlessness came from. My childhood was filled with arguing, yelling, and fighting within the house. It wasn't my mother's fault; she did the best she could with what she had at the time. Even her exposure to the abuse of our fathers over the years created an unhealthy approach to how we as a family communicated. During the course of my adolescence, my Ritalin prescription was adjusted by the doctor several times.

While in school I guess I could say I benefited from the medication, but maybe that was because I just didn't know any better. My behavioral issues as a child were more of an outcry for attention due to the trauma as a child. My mother didn't know any better; she was going by the guidance of the doctors. Turns out I don't think the doctors even knew that I was reacting to my traumatic childhood experiences. My behavior was a coping mechanism, and as a result, I was medicated with Ritalin from age seven to seventeen. Summers growing up seemed to be better because I remember not having to take the medication as much.

As a child I felt that I needed to take this medication because something was wrong with me. I can recall a time in my life when I believed the MD on the back of the pills stood for Mentally Dumb. I had to have been eight or nine at the time, yet that was how I felt about myself. I used to tell my mother I hated my life and I wished I were dead. I wished I had never been born because of the pain I was feeling inside. I felt trapped and didn't know how else to express what I was experiencing. I said so many hurtful things over the years, especially during my years of active addiction.

I carried those resentments because my ego didn't want me to let go and admit my wrongs. It was through the twelve steps that I was able to identify and admit these things. I wasn't able to truly dig deep into the healing process of my recovery just by utilizing the twelve steps alone. I needed therapy. Prison alone was a traumatic experience for both Shannon and me individually. For the majority of people in the world who have been incarcerated, it's a traumatic process whether they want to admit it or not.

The beautiful thing about our relationship was that families that were once torn because of addiction and incarceration have now been brought together to celebrate a beautiful story of God's grace and favor. Leading up to getting married, Shannon and I went to pre-marriage counseling as a requirement through the church. We then took marriage counseling after the fact. At first, going to marriage counseling seemed a little unnecessary, maybe even excessive, but it was worth it. We hadn't had any serious issues prior to marriage, but the greatest thing about it was that I married my best friend.

The church we got married in was the same church my navigator brought me to when I first came home from prison, Reynoldsburg United Methodist, which was where I helped make Kairos cookies. I stood at the altar and looked into the crowd of guests there to support Shannon and me. I was speechless to see her in her wedding gown being led down the aisle by her father. She was stunning, and her smile had her glowing the whole way up to me. I stood there as I waited for her, thinking about how we had met and everything we had been through in life. At that moment I whispered, "Thank You, God."

We are not perfect by any stretch of the imagination. However, she has the same ambitions and desires as me. We have hopes and dreams for a better life than that of our pasts. My thoughts and opinions are no more important than hers, and together this makes us great for one another. I have bad days and so does she, and we have established a relationship and routine that supports those days when we have our setbacks. I'm still blessed to be able to say that she has always been there to support me, and for that I will forever be grateful.

Throughout our relationship, we have never argued about finances and have always contributed fifty-fifty. At work Shannon went from executive assistant to business manager, and I was still working a lot of overtime. It was hard for me to balance that and find time to write. I have erased and started this book over half a dozen times, but I never lost sight of what I truly wanted to do. She, like me, envisioned more in her life, and yes, it has required more dedication while overcoming the challenges of doing something new for the first time. She achieved new accomplishments in her own life as well by acquiring her human resources SHRM certifications.

The SHRM certification is for individuals who perform general HR and HR-related duties. These are the only human resources certifications offered by the world's largest HR membership organization. This was a huge accomplishment for her as only 30 percent pass this test the first time around. She proved to be in that 30 percent bracket. My whole life my biggest challenges have been based on my own personal struggles with self-doubt and negative self-talk. I really am my own worst enemy, and sometimes I don't even realize I'm doing it.

Thoughts and feelings centered around not being good enough, questioning why I have to work so hard to get ahead in life, plagued me for as long as I could remember. I was under the impression that life shouldn't have to be so hard. I don't mind working hard; that's not what I'm saying. What I'm trying to articulate is that trading so much of my time to make money just didn't seem to have to be the answer. I began to realize how much time was being taken away from my personal life and my marriage. I was at a turning point with my job and thinking about getting out of the factory and the manufacturing industry altogether. Then, in October 2019 I lost my job.

It was a major blow to me personally. I reached out to my mentor and sponsor to open up about what I was feeling. I took an inventory of where I had gone wrong in my job and what had led to how and why I was fired. Bottom line, the job just wasn't a good fit, and I understand now why companies have criteria in place to ensure they have the right candidate for the job. The mistakes I made consisted of spreading myself thin and not staying organized while multitasking. I learned a valuable lesson about myself when I got fired. I'm not good at multitasking more than four or five things at once in a highly stressful work environment. Because of that, I realized that I should have communicated sooner that I was struggling to meet the requirements of the job.

There were other contributing factors that pertained to management at the time as well. In the end, the most important takeaways were what I needed to realize about myself. It was hard work coming to grips with this when talking with my sponsor and mentor. They helped me see the bigger picture. My mentor gave me the advice to find what I truly loved doing. Easy enough, right? But it's frustrating finding a niche. For so long I'd lived under false narratives of limited beliefs. Now I had to take responsibility for them.

I began to reflect on my year-to-date earnings, and I quickly realized I had two hundred hours of overtime and had grossed $60k by October. Even though it doesn't seem like much time, looking back on it, I realized that I was always working. I would go to work without knowing whether I would be working eight hours or more. Having to wait all week to find out if weekends were going to be mandatory seemed like a prison within itself. After being fired, I began digging into writing my book again and thinking about new job ideas. How could I establish a more balanced life that would be rewarding financially and provide freedom of time? I loved the idea that I was given an opportunity to reinvent myself.

It wasn't too long before I found a job in sales with a residential heating and cooling company. It really opened up new financial opportunities because the commission was good, and I was home more. I can't say that I liked what I was doing, because I wasn't passionate about it. The money was good, but it wasn't what I was truly called to do. That fall I had a random phone call from Mark asking me for help. Apparently, he relapsed and needed a ride to get his vehicle because he had loaned it to a drug dealer for dope, and he was getting evicted from his apartment. After I picked him up, he broke down and told me about his using.

I took him to get his vehicle, and when I was dropping him off, he asked me to wait because his car wasn't there at the house. I waited five minutes, and when he got back in the car, he asked me if I would take him back to where I picked him up. Whoever had his car wasn't there with it. Something didn't feel right about the whole situation. As I asked Mark what was going on, a guy ran up and started banging on the passenger side window where Mark was sitting. The guy pulled a gun out and pointed it at Mark's head. I ducked my head, threw the car into drive, and sped off.

On the highway, I started yelling at Mark and expressing my frustrations with him. "You come home from prison, start using drugs again, ask me for help, and almost get us shot? Mark, we are done. I'm taking you back, and don't call me again until you're in a sober living house. You jeopardized not only me but both of us!" During the car ride back, I didn't say a single word to him. The last time I saw Mark was when I dropped him off at the gas station across the street from where I'd picked him up. After I dropped Mark off, I called and told my wife about everything. Needless to say, she was pissed with me. I asked her, "How was I supposed to know that this was going to happen?" She was more than upset. She was angry because I could have been killed.

Despite that unexpected life lesson, things were going well for us at home. The year 2020 came around, and in February I got more sad news. My sponsor from prison, Terry, passed away from an overdose. I learned that when Terry was released from prison, he moved back home to help his parents, and things got rough. He ended up using again. Next thing I knew, I found out he had passed away. I just thought about all the programs he had helped with in recovery while I was in prison. I thought of how much of an impact he made in my recovery, not to mention all the other people I knew he affected in a positive way.

Finding out about his relapse and his being back in jail was shocking news. He was the last person I would ever expect this would have happened to. Because of his love for Christ and recovery, I just didn't ever think that he would go back to his old ways again. The tragic grips of addiction tell a deeper story than that of just a relapse. It's a life of torment and pain. When not resolved, nobody is above the irreparable outcomes that are sure to follow a relapse.

Sometimes you get another shot at it. Other times, unfortunately, your life ends with tragedy. Families are torn, and they are left to pick up the pieces. All the while, they try to make sense of their own lives, with your absence as a constant reminder. All I can do in situations like this is pray for God to comfort their families and help them find closure during their time of grieving. I can't just sit back and think to myself, *Ohh... that's sad.* and not do anything. That's why I pray for them. I've had to reflect on the passing of so many people in my life that I now have this approach to how I deal with such unfortunate news.

It helps me with grieving as well. I find time for myself away from distraction. I meditate to quiet my mind and pray. I focus on the feelings of love and comfort. I pray that that feeling is delivered to the families and to those who have passed away. I pray to God, asking to guide them. I pray for their souls that they are able to recognize that it's God guiding them. Dealing with so much death in my life reminds me of the first time I heard the analogy that using drugs was like walking a fine line between life and death. It's so true.

When I spend time at the headstones of Big Country and Cody, I think about the memories I have of them. I'm reminded that I have to make the best of this life to honor them. I know it's what they would want. To me their graves are a sanctuary, because it feels like I'm closest to them while I'm there. It pains me even though I know they are at peace. Then I'm reminded of the opportunities that were missed and how I can do things differently in life. I find myself taking a deep breath when coming to grips with it all. I know I'm still able to do better with my life, which is what they would want.

What would I want for them if our roles were reversed and they were the ones visiting my headstone? I would want them to get up and make the best of life. I would want them not to be sad, because I see a life filled with opportunities for them to experience. I would want them to go and do the best they could and be a blessing to someone. That's what I would want. I would thank them for the frequent visits, and I would thank them for taking the time to clean my stone. I would tell them how amazing heaven is, and I would assure them that I was okay.

After all, isn't that what we want for ourselves and our loved ones? A pureness of peace that is so deep in comfort that nothing else can exist because it's eternal? Those are the desires that I seek for myself, my family, and my friends. No more pain.

As we are all too familiar, 2020 was a year that the whole world will never forget. The year of the "Big C." As I shared earlier, I was doing sales for a residential heating and cooling company. As the whole world was glued to the television watching the pandemic unfold, I was out making money and talking to homeowners about the unprecedented times.

Leading up to that, Shannon and I had decided to try and get pregnant. We prayed about it, asking God to give us a sign if that was the direction He wanted us to go. We were uncertain about whether or not we should try and have a baby. Shannon prayed, "God, if this is the direction for our lives, show us a FROG."

I said, "A frog?"

She replied with a smile, "Yeah, Fully Reliant On God." My mind was blown by the unique and beautiful approach she took with this amazing request.

Now here's where, as a reader, if you have questioned any of my content so far about God, the universe, and the Law of Attraction, things should change your mind. Shannon and I believe that we have the ability to create any and all possibilities in our lives through our faith in God. I'm sure you're thinking, "It's easy to get pregnant," and that's fine. I agree with that, but to ask for a specific sign? Now we're getting specific.

Not to mention the doctor telling us it could take up to a year because Shannon had an IUD taken out, and we were also older. Shannon was thirty-eight, and I was thirty-nine, knocking on forty's door. So Shannon asked for a frog as a sign, and until then, we couldn't remember the last time we saw one. Over the course of the next few weeks or so, we continued to pray and worked on envisioning a frog in our lives. Remember, everything is vibrational, meaning everything has a frequency—our thoughts, our intentions, everything.

Weeks went by, and as I was scrolling through Facebook a friend of mine posted a picture from the great state of Florida. In his picture was a frog. In the post it stated Florida frogs are different from Ohio frogs. I sent the post to Shannon and asked, "Well… does this count?"

Naturally, she was excited and said "yes."

About a week later Shannon saw a frog, and before you knew it, we were seeing frogs frequently and sharing them with one another as we would see them.

It wasn't long after that that we found out she was pregnant. Actually, it took a month. Shannon's IUD was taken out in February, and we found out she was pregnant in March. We started planning and thinking of names and all the things that couples do to prepare. It's funny to think back on it all because when we both met, we didn't want a kid. Shannon already had a child and didn't want to start over again, and I just wasn't sure.

Yet after getting married and talking and thinking about our life together, the idea of a child sounded more realistic and practical. Well, what about COVID? Yeah, we were unsure about the news from the pandemic, and everything was on a day-by-day basis for us.

As I said, the whole world was on lockdown and glued to the TV, watching for any kind of positive development. We didn't know what to expect. Shannon was working from home, and by spring I was classified as an essential worker. Like so many others wearing masks, I was also wearing gloves while going into people's homes. I was busy, and at first money was good, but then everything drastically changed. I began to get fewer and fewer hours, and it finally got to the point where I was only working ten hours a week because sales were down.

During all this, I met a homeowner who happened to be a police officer, but not just any officer. This guy oversaw high-profile motorcades—think celebrities, politicians, and even the president. We got to talking, and he saw me for who I was now, not my past, which really stuck with me, a quiet reminder of how far I'd come. Those homeowner chats were all rewarding, but I was still deeply searching for my next step in life.

Around that time a friend of mine in the Iron Workers Union mentioned they were looking for people. It was steady work, and I had to make a choice because now there was a baby on the way. It was good money and great insurance, and so I went for it. I took the test, passed it, and switched jobs just like that. My first major construction job was helping build the new Columbus Crew soccer stadium. The guys I met that year welcomed me with open arms. There were no judgments, just complete support with one goal in mind: get the job done. My job at first was to learn hand signals to communicate with the crane operator and learn how to rig steel beams to the crane.

I literally watched the stadium get built from the ground up. This was by far the hardest yet most rewarding job I had ever had, and I was proud to admit that. Working with the ironworkers in Columbus, Ohio, pushed me to an all-time high in my personal life. I was mentally and physically challenged each and every day. There is nothing easy about ironwork, as you're constantly on the move. Whether you're connecting the steel, walking the iron, or following behind to finish bolting the steel beams to columns or welding, it's nonstop work. It was an interesting and impressive process to watch and learn.

I just remember thinking to myself that I should have gotten into commercial construction years earlier. There was a sense of pride that came with this line of work. Looking around and knowing that what you're doing is contributing to the development of our country's infrastructure was a great feeling. By June, Shannon and I found out we were having a baby boy. I remember coming home from work, and Shannon had a smile on her face as I walked in the door. She gave me a little gift bag, and as I opened it, I found a little blue newborn onesie that said *Baby Boy* on it. I was so excited! I immediately thought about my family and sharing the news with everyone.

The name we had picked out if it was a boy was Elias, a biblical name. It's the variant of Elijah, and the meaning is: "The Lord is my God." In the Bible, Elijah was a prophet and also referred to as Elias. Elias was seen talking to Jesus on the mountain in the parable of the transfiguration. This is where God came and revealed Christ as His son to the prophets. A special name for a boy gifted to us from God. I had no doubts in my mind: Elias was going to bless us and all who met him.

During Shannon's pregnancy, I regularly prayed over her health and Elias's health. I could feel God's presence in our lives, keeping us safe and healthy, especially during COVID. Long workdays turned into long workweeks while we worked on the new stadium. This was a normal routine by now, which was to keep ahead of the deadline. In July, when I was rigging a piece of iron to the crane, my finger was pinched between two steel beams on the ground. I could have lost my whole finger, but instead it pinched the tip of my finger and separated the nail from it. I went to the ER, and the doctor just reattached the skin and wrapped it up.

I went back to work the next day and kept rigging. Eventually, I was given an opportunity to learn how to weld and walk the iron to finish bolting the steel together. By the grace of God, no bones had been broken in my finger. When school first started I was taking night classes, and then in the fall the school switched to weekly blocking. They started a new class schedule where one week a month I left working in the field to be in school eight hours a day and had to file for unemployment. Shannon had her last ultrasound the week school started with the new schedule. I tried to switch the weeks around so I wouldn't miss the ultrasound. I reached out to the school and coordinated a month in advance about the issue.

The school wouldn't make an exception. I explained why I needed to switch, but I was told to either miss the ultrasound or lose my spot in class and come back in the spring to start over. They had a zero-tolerance policy, which I felt was a harsh ultimatum. At this point in my life I wasn't going to miss anything that had to do with my family. I talked it over with my wife, and in the end I chose my family, so I notified the union of my departure. To be honest with you, in the end it was a great learning experience, but at forty years old I realized that this was a young man's career.

I'm not saying I'm old, but if you get into ironwork, you need to do it earlier in life so you can retire at forty, not the other way around. I thought about it and realized that there were plenty of other opportunities in life, plus I still needed to finish writing my book. My time with the ironworkers will always be one of the most memorable jobs I've ever had. Some of the hardest workers I've ever met and worked with were on that job. I can look back and say I helped build and touched every steel beam on the east side of that stadium. When I withdrew from the ironworker's apprenticeship, I spoke with my Uncle Doug about it. He had been plumbing for over thirty years, so I asked him about work, and he was able to get me an interview with his company.

I decided to stay in commercial construction because I truly enjoyed being outside and working with heavy equipment. During my interview, I explained that I was trying to find my place in the trade industry and that I didn't want to go back to factory work. I explained that my wife and I were expecting a baby at the end of December, and I used personal references that spoke of my character. I even referenced previous employers to support my work ethic. By the end of the interview, I got the job as a commercial plumber.

Coming home from prison and trying to find work is hard. You have to have a level of professionalism to get anywhere in life. You can't just stroll into a job and expect to get hired. You have to advocate for yourself, and the only way to do that is by building a resume that supports the qualifications for the role you're looking to fill. Don't get me wrong, there are plenty of employers out there that are willing to train you, but you have to ask yourself: Are you willing to do whatever it takes to make it to the top?

I'm truly grateful for the organizations that have helped me find employment. I highly encourage people who are struggling to find a better means of employment to utilize the resources offered in their communities. Programs such as Job and Family Services are in every state. Do internet searches for fair-chance employment, and also attend job fairs to find other potential job leads. If you're in Columbus, reach out to these fair-chance employers: Engineered Profiles, Franklin International, Iron Workers Union, and other trade unions. Regardless of adversity, nothing can stop you from reaching your true potential when substantiating your willingness for positive change.

What I mean is, there is no amount of pain and suffering that can limit you from your true potential when you never give up on the vision you have for a better life. There will always be opportunities in life as long as you don't give up on yourself. I'm living proof of this, and it's a testament to the perseverance I've achieved from all my setbacks. It was bittersweet leaving ironwork because of all the hard work I had put into it. In the end I knew that it was just part of my journey as I continued to find my place in life. Doing ironwork made me a better person, and I will always remember what went into being out there with those guys building that stadium.

When Shannon and I went to her last ultrasound of Elias, it was a 3D photo. In it Elias was giving us a thumbs-up, which was just another sign from the universe that everything was going to be fine. On December 28, 2020, Elias was born at nine pounds, thirteen ounces, and twenty-two and a half inches long. A healthy baby boy, so precious and strong. He came into our lives with eyes wide open and fully vocal.

    I thought I was ready to be a father. I thought I knew what I was going to feel as I anticipated holding him for the first time. I'm here to say nothing prepares you for the first time you hold the miracle God so graciously blesses you with. When you hold your child for the first time, it's life-changing. In that moment as I held Elias, I prayed to God and spoke a hedge of protection over his life. I prayed, "Thank You, God, for blessing us with abundance, health, and favor." In that moment our lives changed forever.

7.
Divine Timing

Bringing Elias home was nothing short of exciting and scary. For the last ten months Shannon and I had been preparing and acquiring the necessities needed for his arrival: a baby crib, baby clothes, a stroller, car seats, blankets, toys, and everything in between that we thought was necessary. Now he was here and it was time to take our baby home. I went to the car and drove around to pick up my wife and son. I found myself overwhelmed with joy. While sitting in the car as it warmed up, I sat there asking God for strength.

Deep down I knew my intentions for my family were pure, but I didn't know how to raise a child. I was happy but laughingly crying as I said, "God, I have no idea what I'm feeling right now. I've never done this before and I need you." With Covid still prevalent in everyone's lives and you add a newborn baby into the equation, you find yourself thinking of doing everything differently. Twenty-four hours after coming home from the hospital with our son, we already had our first pediatrician visit scheduled.

The visit turned into us taking a trip back to Children's Hospital for jaundice. At Children's Hospital we were told that we both couldn't go in together due to Covid protocols. Shannon looked to me for advice, not knowing what to do. Who was going to go in with Elias? She was too weak to carry him in so I took him in and then the doctors let us switch out. I definitely voiced my frustrations with that policy. You had hundreds of thousands of people out shopping in stores and malls.

You mean to tell me we can't go into the hospital together with a newborn when we just came home from the hospital twenty-four hours prior? Shannon was crying and I was frustrated. We didn't know about infantile jaundice. I just wanted my son to be okay and for my wife to be comfortable.

After several hours Shannon and Elias were finally admitted to Children's Hospital. I went home and grabbed some necessities for our stay. It was a very tense experience for both of us having to go through this whole ordeal. We had to keep Elias under a UV light for two days to help break up the bilirubin that his liver was working on breaking down.

While in the hospital we talked with our family and hospital staff and learned more about jaundice. Jaundice occurs because babies have a high number of red blood cells in their body and the liver isn't processing them quickly enough. This is usually caused by not eating enough or bruising during pregnancy, but there are other more serious causes of jaundice in a newborn. For us, it was due to bruising. Elias was a big baby, and the delivery was hard on him and Shannon. We were in delivery for fourteen hours, and Shannon had contractions every bit of twelve hours. Watching my son's birth was a once-in-a-lifetime experience. Nothing could have prepared me for it; it's just something you have to experience to understand.

As I walked back into Children's Hospital that night, I asked God why this was happening. I tried to come to grips with what was taking place in our lives, and that's when I was hit with a revelation. It occurred to me that there were families in this hospital who would happily trade places with us in comparison to their circumstances. Outside I could hear a helicopter coming in for a landing, and it made me think of the potential outcome of that flight. Was it a life flight, an organ transplant, or an emergency where lives were going to be changed forever? I began to thank God for the revelation and for the hedge of protection over Elias's life. I knew our situation was small in comparison to other families dealing with life-threatening matters such as cancer and other irreversible health conditions.

Two days is all it took for Elias to be cleared to come home. Those two days seemed like a month. We were practically running to the car to get as far away from that place on the day he was released. We just wanted to be home with our precious baby Elias. Our first month home with our child was amazing. I can say the hardest part was operating on little to no sleep. Every piece of advice we heard and read said, "Rest when the baby rests."

I thought I knew what tired was, and then we had a baby. I was used to working long days and being on night shifts and having physically demanding jobs. None of that compared to having a baby. It doesn't matter who you are or how tired you think you may be, having a baby will change that perspective real quick. Waking up every hour and a half to feed and change him was extremely demanding. Slowly over time, he began to sleep longer through the night. It's one of the most challenging and rewarding experiences in life.

Watching Elias grow and start to lift his head and begin rolling for the first time was very momentous for us. I would say my biggest challenge with being a dad was learning to balance my emotions when it came to him bonding with me. He would let me hold him, but it just wasn't the same experience as when Shannon held him. The connection between baby and mother is so deeply rooted. Our first attempt at going for errands as a family took all day for us to get out of the house.

Looking back on it all now, it was actually comical, because now we are out the door in no time. There came a point where Shannon and I both had to go back to work, and it was a challenging turning point. I started back to work before her, and I developed a routine. When Shannon started back to work is when it got a little harder. She went through separation anxiety and then postpartum depression. We went back to marriage counseling, and it was one of the best decisions we made for ourselves. The insight through our sessions validated that what we were experiencing was completely natural and normal. Having Elias in the equation was just a new chapter in our lives.

It was taking more effort to accommodate each other's needs now. Before Shannon ever got pregnant we had a game plan about who was going to watch Elias when we had to go back to work. My family lived two hours away, and the only other person we had was Shannon's mom. We asked her early on if she would be willing to commit to watching him for us during the day. She was thrilled to find out we were considering having a baby, and naturally she said yes to watching and caring for him. It's really because of Shannon's mom that we were able to make this work out. I couldn't envision taking Elias to a daycare and having a complete stranger watch him. I know parents have to do it all the time, but that's just not the direction we wanted to go if we didn't have to.

Ultimately for both of us, if Shannon's mom would not have been able to watch Elias, we probably would have just decided not to have a child altogether. Having a baby and understanding their needs was something I had to learn to do. There is no instruction manual that comes with a baby. Routine pediatrician follow-ups and experiencing his developments were all new. Learning what milestones were and what developments to keep an eye out for was eye-opening. We created this life, and we are watching him develop and evolve. If I were to sum up Elias's first year of life, I can do it in three words: IS THAT NORMAL?

At about six months old Elias was diagnosed with Brown's syndrome, also known as a lazy eye. For Elias, though, the tendons in his eyes were too tight, causing a misalignment. As a parent, the only thing you want for your precious child is for them to be safe, perfect, and healthy. I struggled with this because at first we were not sure if it was just the alignment in his eyes or if it was his vision as well. I went down a rabbit hole while reading and learning about his condition.

I can tell you from firsthand experience that Google is not your friend when looking up medical conditions regarding children. I say this jokingly now, but I was a nervous wreck at first. Shannon really helped me through all of this. She was stronger than me when dealing with the doctors. I went through a phase of deep emotions around Elias's diagnosis, praying and asking God to heal him and keep his sight good. It was a dark time for me, because I felt like we were being attacked.

I struggled with old thinking patterns, and I was able to identify them because of my recovery. I was able to admit in therapy that there was a lot of personal frustration in my life. What I was experiencing was absolute thinking, where I was angry with the hospital for the jaundice. I was resentful of the hospital where Elias was born because of their Covid policy. We were discharged one to two days sooner than normal. I thought that if we had stayed an extra day they would have been able to catch the jaundice. I know now this was irrational thinking, but at the time those were my struggles.

My irrational and emotional thinking allowed me to fear the worst, which is called awfulizing. Because of it, I was creating more stress in my life than what was necessary. I needed to get to the core of why I was struggling. I knew my family needed me, and this stress was stealing my joy. Covid messed everything up for the whole world. With the limitations during lockdown, I wasn't working out as much as before. I hadn't been to the gym in six months. I was just working and coming home and tending to my family. Through taking a personal inventory of myself, I was able to look at my life and identify the gaps in my personal development.

Getting back into journaling and writing and going to the gym after work brought stress relief back into my life. Shannon and I have developed a partnership as parents now. That alone has brought us closer together than the day we got married. It's because of self-healing and therapy that we are able to work on ourselves individually and together. That summer I turned the Big 4-0. Shannon threw a surprise party for me, which was really special. A lot of people showed up whom we hadn't seen for a while. Everyone at the party was in some way or another part of our support system.

One of the largest contributing factors to our success outside of God has been from our support system. Since as far back as preparing to come home from prison it's been about building a support system. It's such a joy to be around people who are happy to see you and who make you happy. To me this is the most rewarding part of having a support system. At some point they become more than just support; they become family. I've never lost sight of where I've come from. I remember when nobody trusted me, and I remember the times when I could barely stand looking at myself in the mirror.

That's not the case now. I love my life, and I love who I've become. The fact that I'm a husband and a father is a miracle. Today I can look in the mirror and smile and believe the positive affirmations that I tell myself. The key to a successful recovery and release from prison is the understanding that you can't do it alone. It's okay to ask for help. For the longest time my personal approach to figuring out life was: I did this on my own; I can figure it out on my own. This is the mindset I had because as a child I was never taught how to ask for help.

My father wasn't there to guide me, and my stepfather only belittled me and degraded me if he wasn't beating on my mom or me. If I made a mistake, I was punished for it. He never talked to me with words of encouragement. I got my butt cracked with whatever he could get his hands on. More times than not it was his belt. By default, my approach to figuring life out was on my own. I didn't really communicate with my mom about these issues.

When I was younger, I took my Ritalin and thought that that was going to help me. Switching doses was emotionally draining and an emotional hell. Psychologically, I was depressed, and it caused emotional mood swings. I would be angry, sad, depressed, and in what I referred to as a zombie state. Changing doses and taking it several times a day messed with me. I was skinny for my age, and early on I remember experiencing hives all over my body from time to time. It wasn't until I got older that the doses were figured out. Once in high school I started to notice I didn't need the medicine as much.

Eventually I stopped taking it altogether. During that time I had a mental and emotional breakdown from it. I was already smoking weed and drinking, which I realize now wasn't the best choice. I know that it all played a part in my emotional development. Coming off Ritalin was rough, and the drugs and alcohol didn't help, but I wanted to fit in and I didn't realize until later that I wasn't even thinking for myself. I was just going through the motions. Looking back on it now, I realize a lot of my struggles could have been avoided had I asked for help. I just didn't know who to trust to talk about my past.

When Shannon's son came to visit that summer, we packed the family up and drove to Myrtle Beach for a week. Our time in the Carolinas was absolutely wonderful, and the drive through West Virginia and Virginia was beautiful and relaxing to see. That week really brought us closer together as a family. It gave me time to relax and unwind. I took morning walks on the beach, and it was the first time I had tasted the ocean saltwater since I was a child in Texas. This was also the first time I had traveled out of state since coming home from prison.

For some reason my parole officer would not allow me out of the state of Ohio while I was on parole. I never asked why; I was just always denied. When Big Country died, I had to bring the funeral program back from his funeral. I was only allowed a twenty-four-hour pass to stay at my mom's house. For whatever reason the parole officer I had was just very strict about me staying in Columbus. I remember seeing guys come home from prison who had life sentences leave the state on vacation. Yet I wasn't allowed to travel. I personally thought it was extreme, though I looked at it as a temporary issue.

Watching guys with life sentences whom I knew in prison come home was priceless. Life was coming together not only for me but for others as well, and it was an amazing experience to witness. For us as a family, the best thing about this revelation is that Shannon and I are breaking generational curses by raising Elias differently than how we were raised. September was a month that I could never have expected. One day after work I was grilling food when I received a phone call from Ryan, Big Country's youngest brother. He told me his mother had passed away.

I was completely shocked. I asked him what had happened and he said health complications. I never would have imagined getting that phone call from him so soon. I asked if there was anything I could do to help and he said, "Thanks, but no." I thought about my family, most importantly my mom, and my heart really just goes out to him and his whole family. How can you put yourself in someone's shoes who has lost their family? I asked him how he was handling everything. He said he was okay and told me he had still been clean since 2017. I told him I was proud of him, and he said "thanks," but other than that he just didn't really have many words. He was just calling to let me know.

I thought to myself, *I just don't understand why there has to be so much death in life.* I finally returned to my mom's a few weeks later. While I was there I went and visited Big Country, Cody, and now their mother at their family plot. I just sat there quietly because I had no words, just sorrow for the whole family. The last twenty years had been absolutely filled with affliction for this family. I prayed for her as I visited Big Country and Cody before I went home. Later that month I celebrated ten years clean from heroin, and I took the day to reflect back on my life. I thought back to all the moments I could remember that were defining to me.

One particular conversation comes to mind from when I was in Pittsburgh. I had a neighbor, and at first I didn't know it but this neighbor was a pastor. It was over time that in passing we would talk. On that particular day while talking, he told me he was a pastor. That day was special for me because of what he said during that conversation. He said, "Son, God's plans for you will always come to fruition. If your purpose is to walk on the right side of the street and during your whole life you choose to be on the left, in the end you will eventually walk on the right side."

I understood what he was saying even though I disregarded it at the time. Looking back on it now, I know that my neighbor was aware that I wasn't living right. I had people coming and going from my house all the time. Even though I never caused any problems, I know that my neighbors knew. Thinking back on everything now, I guess it's safe to say God's plan has come to light. September 23 is a great day and also a sad day for me. It's hard to imagine that Big Country has been gone since 2016 now. It's hard not to take time and think about what's most important to me. I have to hold on to the things that mean the most.

A part of me feels that I have to make up for lost time. Then other parts of me feel like even though I was incarcerated, I didn't miss anything at all. I'm right where I'm supposed to be. That same month I received a phone call from another friend telling me Mark had died. After dropping him off that night, he never got help and he continued to smoke crack. He lost his construction job and reverted back to robbing people for money. Mark attempted to kidnap a woman in the parking lot of a grocery store.

The woman was able to get away, and Mark was eventually arrested. While in his jail cell Mark hanged himself. He had never gotten the help he needed. In the end, he killed himself. There have been many instances where I have known people who continued to struggle with addiction only to either pass away, as my book has shown, or eventually get help. I think back, and there is a long list in my life that is filled with people I knew who have now passed away. It's sad, but how else am I supposed to feel?

"What if?" is a plausible question to ask. What if I had never used drugs? As good as it sounds, it is not logical to ask because this is who I am today. Regardless, the outcome for everyone else who chose drugs would have been the same. Only maybe I just wouldn't have been as close to those who have passed because of drugs. As for those whom I met in prison, I would have never known them. If I had never used drugs I wouldn't have ever gone to prison. That last statement is safe to say because outside of my drug usage, I wouldn't have ended up where my decisions took me because I would have never used drugs.

I'm humbled by where I'm at in my life today, and none of this would have been possible without God. From praying for the first time in my bedroom before I got arrested, to the warm blankets during detox, and even after my release from prison and meeting Shannon... Here I am now, and I have a beautiful son whom we prayed for, asking God for a sign. As our relationship with each other and with God has deepened over the years, so has our understanding of how God speaks to us.

Our belief system continues to grow, and so has our confidence in knowing that everything is going to be okay. My story is proof that anything is possible. We as individuals just have to continue to work on uncovering how God is being revealed to us in our lives. God speaks to each and every one of us in our own unique way. Tapping into that is what takes the most work. Yet once that way is found, holding on to it and not losing sight of it has to stay routine. It's like working out or running or doing a hobby that we love. If we don't continue in it, we begin to lose it.

Eventually, with our son's eye checkups, it came to the point that Elias would need corrective eye surgery. His vision wasn't as much a concern but it still needed to be monitored. The doctor explained to us that we were going to have to start putting eye patches on his stronger eye, one hour a day or two hours every other day. I have to admit, putting an eye patch on a child is disheartening, not to mention dang near impossible. Yet we were able to use the art of distraction by putting the patch on and then taking him outside to play. Every ninety days we had checkups with his eye doctor. Then, in the midst of all that, at ten months old Elias ended up with Covid.

His body handled Covid like it was a cold. A few days later Shannon and I got sick, and that was about the extent of it. Handling the news of Covid was better than my experience with his jaundice and Brown's syndrome. I could see that managing my stress was starting to improve. I thought about Elias and the fact that he had both his parents. It felt good to acknowledge the fact that he already had a better life than I ever did. My father was never there, and he definitely didn't work on himself through therapy.

The number one purpose I have is to provide a healthy home life for my family and to not screw up Elias's personal development. Our biggest concerns during Covid centered around his breathing. All we had to go off of was what the pediatrician told us to keep an eye on. None of the breathing symptoms were experienced. Even going through Covid brought us closer to God. Seeking God's guidance was and is a reflection of our faith, and it's what has gotten me to where I am today. Even though our lives have changed for the better, we are still faced with adversities that are beyond our control. Just because we have faith doesn't mean we are not going to face challenges.

What I've come to find is that it means we are not alone. My tribulations early on in life have given me the confidence and strength to know that God is going to help me get through whatever I go through in life. I wasn't able to truly heal until I was able to completely let go of my past traumas. Getting overwhelmed and allowing the emotional distress to determine the way I reacted to situations that needed to be addressed and uncovered. If not,

I was always going to allow my thinking errors to determine the outcome of my situations.

One of the hardest things I had to come to terms with in therapy was how I handled my feelings and responses to powerlessness. It was through therapy that I was able to identify with my childhood trauma and being powerless. Due to the abuse of my stepfather, I was fearful of him but also resentful of the fact that I never knew my father. The diagnosis of ADHD and being put on Ritalin was also a contributing factor in how I viewed myself. As an adult, because I never healed from that trauma, my emotions were suppressed. I buried this all through active addiction. It was through my incarceration that it was revealed to me how much more in control of my subconscious thinking I was than I had once believed.

A guy in prison once told me, "You have two choices: Deal with the issues in your life head-on, or it's going to deal with you." For once in my life I was forced to stand up and choose a direction. For me that direction was through spiritual and mental meditation. I made many strides early on in creating healthy habits for myself while I was incarcerated: working out, singing, meditating, reading, and learning how God fits in my life. Finding out the benefits of meditation and speaking positive affirmations to myself, along with helping others, has allowed me to grow dramatically. Taking ownership of the fact that I needed therapy was the next leg of the journey in my healing.

Recovery and going to meetings were good for me early on, but as my journey with healing continued, I realized I needed more. When I first moved out of the Embark house and was living on my own, there were times when I would have bad days.

Everyone has bad days from time to time, but I would go to meetings and leave grateful for going. It took an extra amount of effort for me to find a sponsor when I came home. I went through three sponsors in two years as I tried to find someone I could trust and who was serious about working the steps. One died and the other one just stopped working the steps with me altogether. It was during Covid and the birth of Elias that I came to a turning point. It was time for me to dig deeper into myself and not just rely on working the steps.

Talking about and identifying my problems to a group wasn't solving the issue anymore. My issues were no longer about using; my challenges were with how I was handling stress. I wanted nothing more than to absolve myself of all that. This is how I've come to the next leg of my journey in healing. Dr. Gabor Maté said, "Don't ask why the drugs, ask why the pain, in order to get to the root of all the suffering. The disease of addiction is not a disease but in fact it's a trauma response."

Resolving my past traumas has been pivotal for me. I've come to realize that after years of taking classes and identifying my shortcomings, I needed to continue to work on how I was choosing to handle current situations as they arose. If I continued focusing on my past, what good would I be in raising a child? Instead, I've allowed myself the journey to healing. Because of it, I have been able to enjoy life and start a family. Had I not let go, I wouldn't have been able to enjoy a new chapter in life. I wouldn't have been able to see past my addiction. Most importantly, I would not have been able to see past the fence while incarcerated.

In the beginning of this book I explained how I experienced a shift in my mindset. It's because of this new perception that I am here today enjoying life as a father and husband. I realize now that this was God's will all along. Romans 12:2 says, "And be not conformed to this world: *but be ye transformed by the renewing of your mind*, that ye may prove what is that good, and acceptable, and perfect, will of God" (emphasis added). Despite my struggles along the way, being a father supersedes any and all of my past adversities. Being Elias's father has given me the once-in-a-lifetime opportunity to break a generational curse for the English name. Watching him grow, eat new foods, learn to walk, and use words has been the highlight of parenting. He loves being outside, and he loves playing with other little kids.

He knows no stranger when it comes to people. It doesn't matter how big they are. He wants to be in the mix of the entertainment. He is learning to throw the ball and catch. Our faith and confidence that our family is blessed is the approach that Shannon and I continue to hold on to strongly. During Christmas that year Shannon and I went to see the Trans-Siberian Orchestra for the first time, and Shannon's mom watched Elias. That night we also went out to a very nice restaurant in Columbus for dinner called Mitchell's Ocean Club.

It was hands down one of the best seafood experiences I've ever had. Even though it's not in our normal price range for dinner, it was well deserved. It was that evening while eating dinner that I had another revelation in life. It was then that I told Shannon to look around the restaurant. The majority of the people eating there had been there before. This was their lifestyle. This was how they ate most of the time when they went out.

This is the direction of our lives. We have the ability to manifest this lifestyle if we want it. "I'm speaking this into existence for ourselves," I told her. "We can have this too; we're having it now. It's reality now, not just a dream of possibly someday. We're actually eating here. Out of all the people in the restaurant that evening, how many of them have a similar story such as ours in life?"

I'm willing to bet none. So I ask myself again: Why not us? The progression in life is constant, and sometimes you don't even notice the changes because your routine seems almost robotic. It's moments of clarity, such as that night, that have helped me to stop and appreciate what's actually occurring in my life. I hate to use the term "matrix," but at times that's exactly what it is. If you aren't aware of what's going on in life, when do you ever appreciate it? I guess I have the disadvantage of going to prison to use as my advantage in this aspect. The year 2022 arrived, and we were ninety days away from Elias's eye surgery. Work was going really well, and I was working toward my journeyman's certificate in commercial plumbing. The people I work with are supportive and fun to be around. The foremen are good at training and have the patience to teach, which is all I can ask for. I look up to them when it comes to quality work. They don't cut corners, and they take the time to do it the right way the first time and according to revised code. Whether they realize it or not, it has helped me with how I handle my stress at work. This approach shows me how to slow down and not feel the pressure from the general contractor and/or field supervisors. Life hands you curveballs all the time.

As long as you stay focused, perseverance will always be the outcome. I've been able to share my life story with so many people over the years, and the reaction is the same every time. They tell me that had I not mentioned my past about heroin addiction and prison, they would have never guessed that to be part of my life story. Nowadays I don't talk about my past as much only because it's a new chapter. I don't have to live by that story anymore, nor do I have to explain myself. This is the most rewarding part of all of this story: *I don't have to explain myself.*

Whether the guys I work with know it or not, I'm a better plumber because of them. They have shown me the way. Zach, Jimmy, Levi, and Matt, you will always be my plumber brothers. When I first started plumbing, I was unsure of what to expect. Sometimes in construction you're working with people who don't want to teach you. They have horrible communication skills. They are not leaders and are better off working alone, because they are miserable in their own lives. Those types of people are easy to spot, because they are constantly complaining from the moment they show up to work to the time they leave. All I can say is that being placed with people like that creates a long day at work. I focus on positive affirmations more during days that I work with people like that. I also remind myself that I've been through worse, so I know I can get through this.

Perception is everything, and if someone decides they want to be miserable in life there is nothing you can do to please them. I just pray for them, asking for healing in their lives. I'm not going to fall into the codependency of pleasing people anymore. I did it for too long in life. Because of that I lost joy in my own personal life. I work hard because it's just who I am as a person. I have a strong work ethic, and it's something you either have or you don't have. Everything I do, I apply 110 percent of effort, as if I'm doing it for my own mother.

Another challenge I continue to work on in my personal life is dealing with the issues behind "people pleasing." I was always wondering what people were going to think of me. Whether they were going to view me as a failure or not limited me from tapping into my full potential. These issues stemmed from my childhood, and they allowed me to believe that I wasn't good enough. As I discussed, I didn't have my father around, and my emotional development was suppressed by the Ritalin that I was prescribed as a child. I'm now finding myself creating a healthy belief system post-addiction/incarceration.

At work, I do my best and ask questions when I don't understand something. I'm not worried about getting praise from my field supervisor. My purpose is to be at home with my family. The praise I get from my wife and family is all I need in life now. Anytime I'm able to share my story or be a light in someone else's life along the way is a bonus. Aside from raising my son and being a supportive husband to my wife, writing this book has become the second greatest purpose in my life. I believe that by sharing my story I am able to give back to the world what was given to me. Life can be as beautiful as you want it to be even in the midst of dark times. I'm living proof of this and continue to tap into this perception as I raise my son. My hope is to give him a better outlook on life than what I had.

In April 2022 the day had come for our son to have his eye surgery, and as nervous as we were, Children's Hospital was great in helping us that morning. Shannon and I prayed with Elias and thanked God for helping us. We spoke into existence the end result of his healing. I believe that after asking God for something, it defeats the purpose to continue to ask for the same thing over and over again. Once I pray for something the first time, every time I pray after that, I thank God for receiving it. Even if it hasn't materialized into my life yet, the process of manifesting is by declaring it and believing it.

I prayed to get clean, and I got clean. I prayed for a better life, and I have it. I asked for a family and now I have a wife and a son. We prayed for financial freedom, and we are living it. I prayed for direction in life, and I found a career. Life has its ups and downs. I don't want to come across as though I have this perfect life. I am testifying to God's grace and the power of the Law of Attraction. I still have debt, but it's manageable, and we aren't living beyond our means. We have peace of mind and are not living paycheck to paycheck.

I'm older and wiser now, and every day is filled with new challenges, especially as a parent. It's how I deal with the challenges today that define the level of success in my life tomorrow. The scariest experience while raising Elias was when he choked on a piece of food, not once but twice. The first time was while we were at home, and the other time was while we were in a restaurant. Each time he choked, the experience was scary and dramatic. By remembering what we learned while preparing for Elias's birth, we were able to step in and save his life. Both times, his lips turned purple, and we had to clear his mouth out, flip him over on his stomach with his chest in our hands, and pat his back between his shoulder blades using the base of our palm on his back.

Those defining moments erased all my other concerns of self-doubt. Adrenaline was pumping both times, and in those moments, nothing else mattered. I'm doing my best, and I know that it's going to provide for my family. I'm able to rest on that. I no longer have to dwell on the fact that there are felonies on my record. Yes, there are limitations in my life; I can't own a gun, and

I can't hunt using certain guns. I can still fish and I can still travel and go hiking and do so many other things in life that I enjoy.

Today, I have a deeper appreciation for life, more than I ever had prior to prison. Before prison, my outlook was that I was going to die from my addiction. No one should have to live with that turmoil. I realize now that my primary issue was my inability to uncover the pain that was suppressed. I'm not suggesting that my pain is any more important than someone else's. I'm simply emphasizing that this work is essential for anyone dealing with trauma. To understand the root of the trauma, we first need to recognize it. Only then can we properly address what's needed to rewire our thinking and heal. By rewiring our thinking, we are able to break out of our old patterns that have kept us captive for so long.

I couldn't see this until I got clean, and even today as I write, there are still thoughts that remind me of my past. I know the pain associated with that old life, and that pain just isn't worth entertaining anymore. A prime example of the awareness of my struggles is with stress. I used to get mad and blow up when things got hard, and it was because of feeling powerless. When I felt powerless, I shut down because I felt cornered and trapped. I was unable to successfully see the stressful situation through to the end. I'm able to pinpoint when I'm getting stressed now, and I can communicate that I need to take a break from a situation. Like I said, these are just some examples that I addressed during therapy, which you, as a reader, may be able to use or relate to as well.

Most of my stressors are with parenting now because I'm dealing with a two-year-old lizard brain. A "lizard brain" is just implying a small brain; Elias is still developing. He has no rationale when throwing his fits. For example, he's crying because he wants to be picked up. When you pick him up, he's throwing a fit because he wants to be put down. I could have said squirrel-brained, but lizard-brained sounded funnier. In those moments, instead of getting angry when he bites, spits, hits, and throws things, I'm working on not giving him a reaction. It's not a perfect technique, but by catching him before he does those things, I'm able to use the art of distraction to control the situation. I am not giving parenting advice; I'm sharing what I've learned as a first-time parent.

It's not always a perfect outcome, and a lot of the time, he ends up throwing a fit because he's two. He doesn't know how to regulate his emotions yet. I'm able to understand this because I have had to learn how to regulate my emotions after years of emotional repression. My Recovery Services advisor once said, "You are at best a mature seventeen-year-old trapped in an adult body." I was thirty-something in prison at the time with two years of recovery. Randy, if you're reading this, I would hope to have a new diagnosis of a mature thirty-something now that I'm in my forties, married with a child, and over ten years without drugs.

I used to struggle with what success meant for me. I thought it had to look a certain way. That vision for me was based on everything I didn't have growing up and while addicted to drugs. That ideology had to include a nice car, a nice house, and money to travel and go shopping. I understand now that those ideas are all materialistic and superficial in the grand scheme of how true happiness is defined. Those possessions do not guarantee happiness. Don't get me wrong, I have nice things today, and I am grateful for those assets, yet I've gained them through moderation. Materialism does not create my happiness like I once thought it would.

Happiness can be found within each and every one of us. Once I was able to harness true joy, then all the other things in life that I wanted to acquire began to materialize. I have a friend who is a successful realtor, and there was a time when I was considering getting into real estate, so I reached out to him. After explaining to him why I was thinking about taking this career route, he helped me navigate getting to the Department of Commerce to apply. There was a vetting process that needed to take place for consideration because of my past felonies, and in the end, I was still denied by the board. Their reasoning was that due to my past, they felt that I was unfit for the role and didn't meet the qualifications as a candidate.

Regardless of the rejection I received, there was an even more rewarding takeaway from all of this. During those times of talking with my friend J.D., I remember many conversations we had about leadership and the definition of wealth. He asked me what wealth meant to me. I replied with a very basic answer, saying financial stability, money in the bank for retirement, an investment portfolio, a will for my family, and other assets such as a house and a car. He then began to explain to me how, when he was growing up, his father was a hard worker. He had all those things I just mentioned for his family, but he was never home because he was always working. He then told me that wealth to him meant work-life balance and freedom of time. J.D., thank you for opening my eyes to a deeper understanding of what true wealth is.

I valued that conversation, and it soon became apparent to me that the most valuable thing we have in life is time. How am I going to manage my time in a way that I am able to spend more time with my family and loved ones? I'm going to start by working on not letting distractions steal my joy. For me, I allowed the distractions of the things I didn't have to rob me of the things that really mattered. I had a false and unrealistic expectation of what defined me as successful and wealthy. I asked myself:

Am I healthy?

Is my family healthy?

Are we safe?

Am I happy?

Is my family happy?

These are just a few of many things I began to ask, just to help you get an idea of how I was beginning to ground myself. I soon began to see the bigger picture of what true happiness and wealth could be. Sure, I would love to take a vacation to some exotic tropical location with my family or have a big house in the country and own my own business. In time, I truly believe I can acquire the full scope of what is planned for me and my family. I have to start somewhere, and for me, it starts within myself. Today I have insurance, and we both have begun to think long-term for our family's future.

Investing in stocks and buying life insurance policies. Understanding the difference between a 401(k) and a Roth IRA. Getting Elias a life insurance policy now so that as he gets older, he can continue to contribute to his policy. Unfortunately, when I was growing up, these things weren't taught to me; I had to learn about them late in life. Yet I believe there's no better time than the present to educate ourselves, and for that I'm grateful.

There was a time when I thought I didn't want a family, and I definitely didn't want to get married. Nothing else mattered to me but me and my drugs at the time. As my prosecuting attorney once said, I was a threat to the community and my well-being. Those words resonated with me for many years until I was able to truly forgive myself. When thinking about Big Country and his family, I'm forever reminded of how important family is, because it means everything to me. As for him and his parents, it truly shows that. Once they lost Cody, the pain was far greater than finding joy in life. In July 2022 Ryan called me again only to tell me that his father had passed away due to health complications.

To me, I look at it as broken heart syndrome. It reminded me of my grandma and grandpa. My step-grandmother suffered from Alzheimer's for eleven years. My grandpa took care of her at home. He fed her, bathed her, and changed her diapers until, ultimately, she passed away. He was never the same afterward. Every night he prayed, asking God to take him. He would pray, "God, I'm ready when you're ready. I've done everything I can possibly think of that you would have had me do, and I'm ready." It was heart-wrenching to hear him pray this every night. Yet I understood that he had given up. Much like I had done in my life when I was using.

Ryan's family was consumed with so much pain over the years. His mom and dad ultimately lived out the rest of their lives brokenhearted. For Ryan, though, I'm happy to say he's still sober and is breaking generational curses by raising his family differently. Picking up the pieces to his life has now taken on a new meaning, just like me with my family and raising Elias. I have adopted a new meaning in life. Today, Elias has his mother and father, and he isn't being emotionally messed up from the trauma that I once experienced, and the same goes for my wife, Shannon.

We are teaching him how to pray when we eat. He has learned how to say "please" and "thank you." And it's a beautiful feeling knowing that we are healthy. This is just the beginning of our journey as a family. We continue to tap into the unlimited resources that God is revealing to us through the universe. We know that we are stronger today than we have ever been. We are creating new lives for ourselves. It's through meditating on our gratitude and working on healthy communication skills daily that define how wealthy we truly are.

As for Tony and Lewis, my first two roommates at Cedar Point: Well, Tony is in logistics with an agriculture company. Lewis works in hotel and guest accommodations. Both are very successful, and both are raising beautiful families. I don't talk to them as much as I would like, but periodically we reach out to one another just to say "hi." Today, Shane, my friend who also lived with me at Cedar Point and visited with me while I was in Pittsburgh, is a journeyman carpenter. He is thriving in his trade and is still full of energy and extremely successful running his own business.

Like the rest of us, his life has taken on a new meaning as a father as well. My friend Jordan lives in the Carolinas and is a very successful regional quality manager for one of the largest construction groups in the United States. His career has allowed him the experience to travel the country while building some of our country's largest infrastructure. I couldn't be prouder of where his life has taken him.

Jordan, whether he realizes it or not, helped me in life in more ways than one. When he wrote to me while I was still getting processed in Lorain, it was completely unexpected, but it spoke volumes to me. He is more than a friend; he is also Elias's godfather. I couldn't have thought of a better person to uphold that responsibility. All these people are an inspiration to me and a reminder of how unique each one of our lives is. It's amazing how life takes on new meaning as you get older.

I can still think back to my first summer out of high school and remember how clueless I was. No direction whatsoever. Just free-spirited. I still have that quality about me today. It's just structured more around how I raise my son and the energy within my relationship with my wife and her oldest son. It's okay to dream, but we need to have a plan when doing this. How is our dream going to become a reality? What are the steps necessary to get started so that we are able to make the dream a goal and not just some grand idea?

I used to always say, "I'm going to do this and I'm going to do that." I never did anything with those ideas, because I never created a plan. My Aunt Julie once told me, "At what point are you going to stop talking and start doing?" I never lost sight of that, because I applied it once I got clean. I stopped talking and started to take action in life. The saying goes: "Don't talk about it; be about it." Early on, my biggest achievement was getting clean from heroin and staying off it. I started doing the work that was needed to understand why I used drugs in the first place. Without realizing it at the time, I was using drugs because I was hurting inside. My mother did her best raising three kids on her own. Not to mention what she went through protecting us from the likes of my stepfather and father. Both these men traumatized our family, but it was because they were traumatized growing up as well. I don't blame my mother for putting me on Ritalin. I was more than a handful, and there were plenty of other kids growing up who were prescribed Ritalin as well. My coping skills were based on my own set of personal circumstances. As I have shared, my issues had a lot to do with an absent father and an abusive stepfather. I can't begin to imagine the amount of fear my mother must have had moving around to protect her family and at the same time find the necessary means to support us financially.

In my eyes, my mother is a saint, and she deserves to feel safe and secure, especially after all the years of abuse and personal torment she endured. My mother deserves healing as well. Instead, she was left to pick up the pieces as she watched me, her oldest son, struggle with addiction and go to prison. My mother was there for me each step of the way through my incarceration. From county jail every weekend, to Lorain, and several times a month religiously while at Marion. Yes, support is a driving factor when it comes to change. Yet I have also seen both sides of this play out differently. I have seen men with more support than I experienced still relapse and fail upon release from incarceration.

While I was in prison, my youngest brother ended up addicted to heroin, and eventually he lost custody of both his daughters. My sister stepped in and gained custody of the girls. My sister is a social worker and knows firsthand the many degrees of addiction and trauma and how it destroys families and lives. This experience has given her a level of professionalism that sets her apart from most other case workers. Today she is raising our two nieces with my mother. Because of that, the girls are being brought up in a house that is breaking generational curses as well.

My sister and I are closer than before, and I'm grateful to be able to say that. It's taken years of healing for us to get to the point we are at in our lives, and for me, it's a precious gift. Over the years, watching my brother struggle with addiction and ending up in prison was hard. Now he is trying to resolve his financial obligations to the courts through restitution and probation. I don't talk to him as much as I would like; however, I understand he has a life to live as well. Our communication skills aren't the best. When we do talk, it's like we haven't missed a day, even though we may go for three months without talking. He's still trying to figure life out and get past his traumas, which are unique to him.

I can't live life for him. All I can do is stay focused on the purpose I have been given, which is to lead by example. One of the deepest perspectives I have from my incarceration is based on this newfound purpose. I know that I'm a prime example of what change looks like. The men who are still incarcerated whom I stay in contact with are living vicariously through me. I am giving them hope because I'm out here living the dream that they have for themselves as well.

Meditation is key to manifesting and understanding my deepest potential. Christ himself meditated, and it's through meditating that I have become closer to God and my relationship with Christ than ever before. Numerous instances in the Bible talk about Christ going off to meditate and focus on his relationship with God. I believe it was in order to have a deeper understanding of his relationship and true calling. He sweat great drops of blood in the garden of Gethsemane because he felt and understood his purpose to the point of physical conviction. For me, seeing the men who had found a purpose in discipling God's love was an amazing revelation while I was incarcerated. I believe there is no coincidence when it comes to God's intentions and timing. It goes all the way back to the pastor I had for a neighbor in Pittsburgh.

It's up to us what we do with the messages that are being given to us in our lives. Even though my goals continue to change as life progresses, the intended results will always remain the same. Be better than the day before and thrive. I recently read *The Inner Work* by Mathew Micheletti and Ashley Cottrell, which focuses on uncovering limiting beliefs. It's about how your subconscious mind works, and it also covers the process of radical self-analysis. I meditate daily, focusing on positive affirmations, and listen to podcasts when I can from Dr. Joe Dispenza and Dr. Gabor Maté. Shannon and I also utilize Dr. Joe Dispenza's course materials, which include lectures, breathwork, and meditations.

This has helped create a quality of life for us that has provided an undeniably healthier and happier approach to our routines than ever before. Listening to Dr. Joe Dispenza and reading his book *Breaking the Habit of Being Yourself* has been transformative and pivotal in our lives. Also, reading Dr. Gabor Maté's book *The Myth of Normal* as well as listening to his interviews and podcasts has given me a new perspective on myself and how my past choices with drugs triggered responses associated with the trauma in my life as a child. Even with all the support that I have in my life, my reentry was a traumatic experience as I adjusted back to society. This makes sense because prison itself was an emotional roller coaster.

I was just thinking the other day about how hard it was when I first came home and how I felt stuck. The sense of limited opportunities in society because of having felonies and not knowing where to take my first steps overwhelmed me. Had it not been for Kindway Embark and TAPP, finding employment may have been a lot harder than it actually was. Despite these circumstances, I had a desire to work through the adversity that surrounded me. The odds are stacked against everyone coming home from prison, including those who are battling addiction. This is where a support system is highly suggested.

Go to a church and reach out to a chaplain. They are loaded with resources to help get you connected with community programs and organizations. If you're incarcerated and reading this, reach out to your caseworker and advocate for yourself. Get involved with as many programs as possible. Go to the chaplain and ask about classes and programs that provide assistance upon your release. I had to relocate after prison because I knew my town didn't have the support and resources I was looking for at the time. I was willing to sleep in a shelter if I had to, to start over.

Explain to your case worker what's going on and what you're trying to achieve in life. Prisons have a mental health department. It may sound crazy (no pun intended!), but believe it or not, they have a ton of programs and resources. If you're struggling with active addiction, go to a meeting and find out who is chairing the meeting. Explain to them your situation. AA and NA meetings are filled with people who are well-rehearsed in helping a newcomer who is struggling to get twenty-four hours clean. Reach out to a homeless shelter. They have case workers who can help get you in touch with other organizations as well.

Whether it's financial or emotional stress, being able to talk about your challenges and issues helps you navigate through life. Especially when dealing with circumstances such as coming home from prison. Even to this day, from time to time, when I see a prison bus on the highway, I'm taken back to the day I was shackled to another man and driven to Marion Correctional. I'm reminded of the feelings of uncertainty and doubt. I'm reminded of the other fifty or so men who were on that bus with me that day.

Some were repeat offenders, while others were in the same situation as I was, unsure of where life was going to take them and what to expect from prison. When I see a prison bus now, I pray for every single person on that bus, including the corrections officers. I pray that they find God and that their lives are transformed in supernatural ways. Still to this day, from time to time, I find myself overcoming the mounting emotions behind survivors' guilt from my past heroin addiction. When I think back on when I first started using heroin, how did I not see that the morphine pills that killed Cody were the same as snorting OxyContin and fentanyl, which led to shooting heroin?

I realize that while my intentions were never to hurt anyone, my addiction still affected so many people's lives. This realization brought a heavy burden of shame upon me early on in my journey to healing. I've learned to manage this over time by reminding myself that I've done my best over the years to make amends. By staying off heroin, I'm able to do what's called a living amends. Though things could have been fatally different for me, I am reminded of all the other scenarios I survived. I panhandled for cash and passed out under loading docks on the streets of Pittsburgh due to my drug use. I was robbed at gunpoint while buying dope, and I survived prison. I never overdosed, and I never had an infection that caused hospitalization or loss of any limbs from shooting heroin. I never contracted Hepatitis, and I don't have AIDS.

The quality of life I have today is a miracle because I know I've overcome a lifetime of pain. My journey is renewed daily because I know we are not guaranteed tomorrow. This is why I do my best today to make the best out of today. There are so many distractions in life that make it easy to be mad and unhappy. It takes work to set yourself up for a good day. I have learned through this journey that I can set myself up in a positive direction for success. As of March 23, 2025, I have thirteen and a half years without heroin, and that in and of itself is a miracle. I carry this with great pride each and every day because I know I have been blessed.

By focusing on what I have to be grateful for rather than focusing on the materialistic things that I don't have, I have narrowed the path for enlightenment. The little boy who once lost the innocence of his childhood has been reborn through my son Elias, and the same goes for my wife. The little girl who lost the joy of her imagination as a child has been reborn through our son as well. Today, my wife Shannon and I are able to heal together. It's because of these stories that *Emersion* has been created.

This memoir is a testimony for anyone and everyone because we all have dealt with, or are dealing with, some kind of trauma in life. All our stories are unique and should be embraced with motivation to dig deeper into the journey of healing. Every one of us has something positive that we can give to help someone else. I understand that not all people want to entertain the idea of going through the healing process, though. I get it; I was there. For me, the pain felt good to dwell on, and at times in my life, I loved being miserable, because it fueled my addiction. The misery was feeding on me, and the more miserable I was, the deeper the roots of pain were growing inside me.

If we are truly honest with ourselves, though, deep down inside, there is a little flame of desire that wants to be happy. I got that last part from Ram Dass's "Sit Around the Fire." If you were just able to sit alone with yourself and meditate on the thoughts of how joy is defined within your life, what would it feel like? What would it look like? Better yet, what subconscious thoughts would you notice while trying to quiet your mind and focus on those elevated emotions of joy? I highly doubt that you would be able to deny the desire to have that peace in your life all the time. Today I choose peace over torment.

Emersion is my life today. I lived a life of torment and pain, and now I emerge every day with a new perspective. I feel that by expounding on it, someday my story will help change a life. I was blessed with this shift in my perception, and because of it, my life has been changed forever. It wasn't easy, because of all the pain I had to overcome. Because of the work I've put into understanding what healing is, I was able to write *Emersion*. Like I've mentioned, my healing is not complete. I continue to grow daily, and I'm okay with that.

The key takeaway for everyone reading this is that we can't journey through life alone. It's okay to ask for help, and actually, it's to be encouraged. If nobody has ever told you this before, I will be the first to say it: You have a purpose, and you are special and unique. God is going to use you in a mighty way, just as he has used me. I was able to tap into this mind shift through prayer and meditation, and you can do it too. When I see individuals on the streets panhandling and waving at people as they pass by, I roll down my window and ask if they want food.

I don't give money to them only because I know where my intentions were when I was panhandling and using drugs. This is my way to avoid supporting another addiction, and I can still contribute. I remember a time in the fall of 2022. I was on my way to class for my journeyman's certificate in commercial plumbing. It was cold and raining, just about to start snowing. As I was driving through this busy intersection, I saw a guy standing on the median in between traffic with a blanket and a sign, shivering. He didn't have any shoes on, just socks and flip-flops.

In my soul, I felt God speak to me, "What are you going to do, son?" I didn't even hesitate. I pulled into the gas station and bought a hot sub and grabbed the extra pair of shoes I had in the work van. I walked across traffic and gave him the sandwich and asked him if he wanted the shoes. While he stood there shivering, I could tell he was dope sick, and he replied, "Yes, thank you. Just put them over there." He turned, indicating a spot behind him where his belongings were bagged up in clear trash bags. I knelt and told him to give me his foot, and I put the shoes on his feet. When I finished placing the shoes on this man's feet, I prayed with him. I asked God to help this man find a better set of circumstances in life. Whether he was grateful or not, I'm not sure. He did thank me, but he did it while standing there shivering. The man was soaking wet, and it was not a good sight. I didn't do it for a hug or self-gratification. I was just convicted to help.

As I walked back to the van, I couldn't help but cry as I was reminded of how far God had brought me in my life. The issue wasn't just that the guy was standing in the cold without any shoes on his feet; it was deeper than that. My perception had me thinking more along the lines of what got him to this point in life. I don't know if it was an ultimate form of manipulation or not. Regardless, there were underlying issues that this man was dealing with, and I felt a calling to help. Whether it was mental health or addiction or both, this man was dealing with some form of trauma, and in that moment, my heart went out to him.

You don't have to go to prison to be in prison. You don't have to be addicted to drugs to be trapped and consumed by debilitating addictive behaviors. Trauma and mental anguish are life-wrenching in and of themselves. Maybe the act of kindness that I displayed wasn't even for the guy standing in traffic. Maybe there was someone in traffic that day who needed to see God at work. Maybe I saw my past self in that man. Or maybe I was doing for that man what so many loved ones tried to do for me. I don't know; I can only explain it as a strong inner impulse.

That's where I'm at in life today: focused on being in a place where I can hear God more. For those of you who are reading this who are going through addiction, trauma, or a release from incarceration, I want you to know that you can overcome this adversity. I'm not going to lie: It's going to be hard, but it is possible to overcome. It's worth the transformation, but you can't do it alone. Join a recovery group, find a sponsor, and ask for help through community resource groups. Speak to a counselor and investigate learning more about why you are struggling with depression. It is possible to overcome your challenges.

We need to talk about it and find someone to help uncover what we're going through. You just have to remind yourself you're not alone. If you're in jail or prison and you're reading this, I want you to tell yourself that this isn't the end; it's just the beginning.

Like I mentioned earlier, prison is filled with programs and organizations designed to help you prepare for a successful reentry. During my addiction, I always told myself that tomorrow I was going to work on getting clean. Tomorrow never came. We start today.

This is just the beginning of a new way of thinking. This is the journey to healing, and *you are not alone*. You never know how your actions are going to affect someone else in the world. A perfect example of this is when I took a friend out for breakfast one day. This friend had come home from prison, and I wanted to catch up with him. He was someone I knew well in prison, and it was exciting to see him home now. He was now working and living life to his fullest, and I wanted to spend some time with him, so we went out for breakfast and coffee. As we were leaving the diner, a stranger walked up to us from across the parking lot, crying, asking for money and food.

My initial knee-jerk reaction was, "Sorry, man, I don't have any cash. We just finished eating, and we don't have any food." As we got into my vehicle and drove over to the gas station to get gas, I just kept thinking about the interaction we had just had with that guy. Clearly he was upset and desperate. He was crying as he walked away, and I thought about how I had rejected him.

While pumping gas I was reminded of a couple scriptures. Matthew 7:7-12:

> "Ask, and it shall be given to you; seek, and ye shall find; knock, and it shall be opened unto you: for everyone that asketh receiveth; and he that seeketh findeth; and to him that knocketh it shall be opened." And also Lamentations 4:4: Or what man is there of you, whom if

his son asks for bread, will he give him a stone? Or if he asks a fish, will he give him a serpent? If ye then, being evil, know how to give good gifts unto your children, how much more shall your Father which is in heaven give good things to them that ask him? Therefore all things whatsoever ye would that men should do to you, do ye even so to them: for this is the law of the prophets.

Unintentionally, when I rejected that man's request for food, I gave him a stone, and it just didn't sit right with me. I told my friend that I needed to go back and find that man and take him to get some food. So we drove back around the block and found the guy down the street at a bus stop. I pulled over and told the man to get in and that we were going to take him to buy some food. I said, "Tell me what you want to eat, and we will go get it."

I would have bought this man a steak at this point had he said that, but instead, all he wanted was a sub and a gallon of water. I explained to him some of my backstory in life with drugs and incarceration. I also talked to him about my relationship with Christ and how God had spoken to me while getting gas. I explained to him that it reminded me of the scripture I'd just shared. I told him I was sorry for turning him away, because as I saw it, God had given me everything I had asked for in life. So, how was I in any position to tell him no? I was not fulfilling my purpose with what God had so graciously done for me.

With the world the way it is today, I truly believe that we can all separate ourselves from the hatred and work on prioritizing personal time to find healing in ourselves. This practice alone is sure to make life better not only for ourselves but for humanity.

There's more to life than focusing on "what they did" or "what they said" to hurt my feelings. Today, I don't have to accept that energy. I can acknowledge it and reject it all at the same time. If I spend my existence focusing on what's wrong in the world, I will never be happy, and instead, my son will grow up seeing how his father was miserable and always complaining. I was exposed to anger, neglect, and verbal and physical abuse by my father and stepfather as a child. It manifested in my life as trauma. Now, if I teach my son violence, anger, and abuse, how much more will that manifest in his life as he gets older?

Today I have been given this precious opportunity to journey through life by working on healing. I'm able to expound upon it daily because it's become intuitive. My healing will continue for the rest of my life, and it's a beautiful concept. I know I'm no longer shackled to my past thinking and toxic subconscious self-talk of deprivation. Basically, I was slowly killing my spirit through negative self-talk that, at times, I didn't even realize I was doing.

It was going on in the back of my mind. I found this out through meditation and trying to quiet my mind. I realized how hard it was to shut the thinking off. Today, life is filled with an abundance of joy, love, and peace. It's okay when I cry because I'm healing, and I'm fine with that. The amount of joy that is in my life is more than I could have ever expected. With that, I will live the rest of my life, living it out for those who couldn't do so. One way is by doing the things I love.

As of recently, I committed to a seventy-five-mile hike in the Appalachians. I'm excited for this next part of my journey. I have never been on a major hike like this before. A part of me has always wanted to do this, so it was special to me for so many reasons. The most significant thing is how this opportunity came to be. I remember one day when I was out for a hike in the woods, and I decided to stop and just meditate on the sound that the woods had created. I felt so grounded and full of peace. As I sat there and meditated on clearing my mind, an idea came to me to embark on a major hike. I thought to myself, *I need to reach out to a few people that I know are avid hikers.*

Upon completing my hike that day, it wasn't even ten minutes after I left the woods that I got a text message with an invite for a four-day hike. What's astonishing about this is that prior to meditating on this idea, I had never spoken to this friend about hiking before. Like I've said throughout this book, the universe will reveal its purpose for your life when you align yourself in a way that allows you to receive what God is trying to show you. The love that I have come to know in my life now has been given to me through so many people, opportunities, and experiences. Even while I was using drugs, I was receiving this love. I just wasn't able to realize it until I got clean.

My family, friends, and loved ones who have passed away will always be with me in my heart and soul, as I continue on my journey of healing. This mind shift has taken years for me to get to where I'm at today. It's amazing how one decision is all it took for my whole life to be altered. In retrospect, all it took was for me to use opiates one time to lose sight of so much ambition. Although it took years to fully self-destruct, opiates are what did me in. I was already living a life that I took for granted based on how much privilege I had growing up. There are so many stories of people who grew up in far worse environments and went on to be amazingly successful in life. Doctors, politicians, lawyers, business owners, judges, etc.

I chose to use drugs and sell drugs. I know I'm not the only one with stories like mine; I'm just grateful that I have this knowledge now. What started as a story of addiction and a life of limited beliefs has now turned into a story of perseverance. I started training for the big seventy-five-mile hike six months out from the start date. Every weekend I would take a day to hike anywhere from twelve to twenty-four miles, depending on my flexibility with time and family.

In preparation for the hike, I began tracking my mileage and caloric intake while hiking. While investing in new gear, clothes, and shoes, I've come to realize this sport is not cheap and cutting corners on cheaper products is not suggested. I've learned that gear is expensive for a reason, so save yourself the struggle and just get the better gear. During my training hikes and testing out my gear and water filters, I have noticed a deeper connection with myself as I've overcome milestones through endurance. I'm seeing things more clearly than I did before. I am feeling a sense of connectivity and awareness outside that I hadn't realized before.

I have naturally progressed to a point of excitement from what was at first nervousness. Then, on Easter Sunday 2024, a few weeks before my hike, my grandmother passed away. She was a wonderful, caring woman who lived a full life filled with love for and from her family. I was so grateful for her love. To see me come home from prison and to watch me as I started my own family was a true blessing and answered prayers. I can't tell you how many nights I prayed to God asking to keep her healthy until I came home from prison. More so, I'm grateful that she was able to see our son, her great-grandson, Elias, until he was three years old. Those memories have made lasting impressions on all of our hearts. It's never easy losing loved ones. Yet in my faith, I know that this journey with our soul doesn't end with our 3D perception here on earth. Our understanding of eternity is finally revealed when our earthly time ends. I know my grandmother is looking down with the rest of my friends and loved ones.

As my hike began at mile marker 70, so did her eternal hike. She's on the next leg of the journey. A new hike, one that is everlasting. My drive to Pennsylvania to meet the rest of the hiking group brought back a sense of youth. To me, it was knowing that I was leaving with anticipation but would be returning home with more knowledge and perspective to help me journey through life post-hike.

My days on the trail were surrounded by a group of men just as excited and eager as I was. Each day was met with a new wisdom share, followed by logistics on what to expect for the day ahead on the trail. Each evening, we gathered by the fire and completed additional wisdom shares after dinner. Over the course of four days, we all had an opportunity to share stories about our personal lives, reflecting on our experiences and understanding of life. For me, the major takeaway was that despite our differences in family background, faith, careers, and social status, we all had similarities in our upbringings and personal struggles. The significance of it all was our ability to take the traumatic experiences and make the best out of them.

The mantras that I acquired during those four days on the trail have become ingrained in my mind since I've returned. These are just a few that I use regularly.

Peace is in every step.

The hike doesn't stop after mile marker 0.

The sun will rise tomorrow.

Despite our choices in life, the outcomes all fall under wisdom.

At one point during our hike, we were all talking as a group, and the topic of vultures was brought up. The significance of a vulture's purpose on this earth is profound. The vulture is designed to take in some of the most vile, putrid sources of food, feeding on dead carcasses for its survival. The vulture's body is able to digest and transform the diseased meat and turn it into nutrients for itself, without ever getting sick. What's even more amazing is that even the vulture's waste is turned into fertilizer. The body absorbs the toxins and is able to make good out of the bad.

Our lives are a lot like the vultures. We as humans are able to take the putrid decay of this life and still make good out of it. Just an interesting side note: A group of vultures is called a *committee*. Our hiking group took on the trail name the Committee. As our hike was coming to an end, one of the outlooks gave the group an opportunity to appreciate the vastness of our location. In the sky flew a group of vultures. This symbolism was just another confirmation from the universe that the work being done on this journey had become manifest.

As the hike ended, we gathered for food and said our goodbyes. We all left with a newfound perspective for life as our journey continued past mile marker 0. After four days away from traffic and society, coming back into the city was a bit overwhelming while driving. I quickly adapted, but the highway felt aggressive and unnatural, yet it was very rewarding to come home and see my wife and son. It gave me a deeper appreciation for life and realizing how blessed I truly am. My life's story and the sequence of events I have experienced as I've traveled through some of the darkest times in life is a testimony of persistence, never giving up on the pursuit of a better life.

Something to be reminded of as a reader is that the hike—and life—doesn't stop after mile marker 0; the journey must continue. Embrace tapping into the unknown and learn how to separate from your subconscious mind. Learn to understand your energy centers and work on your breathwork. Tap into a routine of blessing yourself with positive affirmations. Find it within yourself to believe that you can be healed and that you can change your life. The key to all this is personal conviction, and last but not least, look into Dr. Joe Dispenza. Our minds are more powerful than we realize. It's because of the work through Dr. Joe Dispenza that I have encountered the most significant results in healing.

We are always growing and evolving, and even though this memoir has come to an end, my journey…this journey…our journey continues one step at a time, one day at a time, one moment at a time. And remember:

Peace is in every step.

Be grateful, be well, and just breathe…

Divine Timing

May this book inspire you as much
as it has inspired me to write.

I've tried so many times to put myself where I belong,
But at times it seemed to me that everything was going wrong.
Sometimes life pulls you along;
Unexpected is the feeling.
It's what makes you strong.
From the time that we are born
Until the day that we grow old,
It's experiences like these that become stories that are told.
It's a lesson for me and a story for you.
In time when you read this,
I hope you'll know just what to do.

www.ingramcontent.com/pod-product-compliance
Lightning Source LLC
Chambersburg PA
CBHW030442090526
44586CB00044B/542